WHEN YOU STOP FIGHTING

THE ROAD YOU'RE ON
IS YOUR OWN ASPHALT

DARYL DITTMER

ISBN: 979-8-9906591-1-7 – paperback

ISBN: 979-8-9906591-0-0 – ebook

ISBN: 979-8-9906591-2-4 – hardcover

This book reflects the author's present recollections of experiences over time. Some names and characteristics have been changed, some events have been compressed, and some dialogue has been recreated.

Coming in 2025!

THE FIGHTING STOPS: (Subtitle TBD)

will be the final installment in the

Stop Fighting, Start Living Series

and is projected for a late **2025** release!

Send me your email and I'll send you an excerpt! or two!

(I expect to be ready to send excerpts by early to mid 2025!)

visit https://www.daryldittmer.com

or email me at

daryl@daryldittmer.com

"When the roots are deep,

there is no reason to fear the wind."

—African Proverb

Dedication

Bonnie Peracca—There are very few people I've encountered in my lifetime who've had a profound impact on me. Bonnie was a client for almost 25 years. She was also a beloved friend and mentor. A beautiful heart and soul; the spirit of a warrior; grace and poise rarely encountered.

I will miss our talks, Bonnie. I will miss you. Rest in peace. Until I see you again.

Deep Gratitude

I truly don't believe I'd be writing books if not for my beautiful wife, Kristina Dittmer. For every step along the journey, from the motivation to start, the drive to keep going, proofreading, editing before the editing, encouraging me to do better, support through the entire process, telling me things she knew I didn't want to hear, etc. etc. Oh, not to mention, getting me to commit to write three books as opposed to the one book I planned to write. Two down.

With all my Heart and Love, Babe. Thank you.

CONTENTS

Introduction

The Fight Will Stop

The journey of change can be difficult, intimidating, and filled with myriad emotions. It can also be the momentous adventure of a lifetime, complete with fulfillment, wonderful relationships, and incredible discoveries.

In my first book, *When I Stop Fighting*, I delved into my journey of addictions, destructive behaviors, and failings as a younger person. Then, into the challenges inherent in my quest to be better. I opened the doors to my life and showed how I failed many times because I wanted you to know that success in life is not linear. I wanted to show you that there were failures throughout every aspect of my journey and how I learned to embrace them over time and with experience. I was fortunate to have trekked from having my head planted in my ass, to what has been an incredibly rewarding and wonderful life. My intent was to show you that it's possible, it's doable, and it's attainable.

In *When You Stop Fighting*, it's your turn.

We'll explore what it is you're likely searching for "out there," as well as how you might be looking to acquire it. Whether it be through addiction(s), attention, hiding, who knows? That's for you to uncover and explore. What's in these pages will help you do that.

When You Stop Fighting is about your story. It is a much deeper dive into the journey of life and how it can be difficult and devastating or breathtaking and gratifying. How difficulty and uncertainty can be transformed into a life that you hadn't before dreamed possible. It will also show you that the decision is entirely yours.

A way to illustrate and understand how you're doing on this journey is to look at your trajectory. How long have you been doing what you do, and if you keep doing those things, where are you headed? Once you take the time to understand where you're going, you can decide how you'd like to proceed from that point. *When You Stop Fighting* will show you how.

From the reasons why you're not getting there, to some signs that you might be off track, this book will surprise you, maybe piss you off, but without a doubt, illuminate some of life's meanderings. This path is not for the faint of heart, nor is this book. It will help you understand the steps you'll likely go through and some of the tools you'll need to collect, understand, and develop as you traverse a new, difficult, and beautiful path.

As you move through and begin to experience your life in a different and rewarding way, the path will get narrower and more challenging. You will need different tools as you develop more strength and openness to change. There will be wonderful lessons along the way, and we will move through those by helping to illustrate what some of the lessons might be.

You will experience successes you were not expecting, and life will begin to open into a breathtaking panorama that you no longer feel the need to control or change. As we open ourselves to the unfolding and expansion of our time on this planet and in the universe, the beautifully simple and sublime will be where we're led. And we will also understand that from this palette, we can paint what we'd like.

At some juncture, the fight will stop. You will truly behold this enchanting existence called life.

This is my hope for you.

CHAPTER ONE

CHASING HAPPY

"Don't break my boat!" said Ted, the owner, when he looked at me for the first time.

Ted was a very wealthy dude and owned a new seventy-foot racing sailboat. I was a blue-collar kid, early thirties, doing things that, to me, felt way, way above my pay grade.

I was invited to be the "grinder" on Ted's boat for Antigua Race Week. Not because I was a sailor or in any way fit for the task from an experiential perspective. I was, though, big, strong, and very difficult to wear out.

I smiled at him. "I guess we'll see."

I was invited by a friend of mine from college whose family was very involved in sailing. Bakes could work the boat like a professional, knew all the vernacular, and was comfortable sailing. He knew I'd be strong enough, agile enough, and care enough to figure it out and do a good job.

The races in Antigua were mostly about drinking, with a little racing in between, although I'm guessing nobody but me perceived it quite that way. In their mind, we were here to race, and they were all here to win.

At that point I was living a very different life from what I'd ever imagined but was still very new to the things I was experiencing. I'd been sober close to fifteen years and found myself doing a lot of things that scared the hell out of me.

That was what I was told to do by people more successful in their lives than me. So I did them.

Everyone's life has the potential to go in innumerable directions. Where we're from, who our parents are or aren't, what they do for a living, where we live, city, country, somewhere in between, all play a role in how we start this life. These beginnings don't dictate where we end up, but our environment, surroundings, friends, neighbors, and the attendant experiences they play a part in certainly get us started and help point us in a direction.

My start was rather ordinary and very similar to many people I've met and spoken with throughout my life. Parents that cared for and taught me and my siblings work ethic, manners, and respect for others; an introduction to religion; an older brother and younger sister to learn from; enough food, clothing, and shelter to keep our family going. Plenty, right? Everything we need for a solid start to this life.

Many of us have probably had a similar start, some with much more and some with much less, but I'd venture to suggest that these basics, give or take, are fairly common in our world and have been for quite some time. Do they work? Do they set the stage for a successful remainder of our life? Is there anything else, and if so, where might we find it? These are the questions I'd like this book to explore and to answer for each of us.

This exploration into ourselves, which suggests we take a brief peek behind the curtain of where we all started this journey, can, in many cases, lead to a very destructive construct entitled "blame." I'll be very frank here: If we're going to grow at all, we must leave no room for blame in our life. Which brings up another important point: We are looking back, briefly, only to acquire a fix on the direction or trajectory of our life from our past, to where we are currently. So, let's peek but not get stuck there. We look to understand, we look in order to ask ourselves questions about how we're going to improve and get better, not blame. Blame is also known as lying down and giving up. Blame is a dead-end road because it takes all the responsibility off us and puts it on someone or something else, which leaves no room for our responsibility to improve ourselves.

There are a lot of things I don't recall having been told in my youth. To be fair, there are likely many things I was told that I either didn't listen to or was too busy thinking I already knew. It's difficult to pay attention and learn when we think we already know. However it plays out, whether we're told or not, whether we paid attention or not, is really of no consequence. We can get caught up in all sorts of reasons why or why not, which really aren't worth a second of our valuable time.

What is worth as much of our time as it is possible to give, is to say to ourselves: "Okay, this is where I started, this is what I got." Rather than the path of judging what "they" could have done better, perhaps our attention could be focused on asking ourselves a couple questions: "Am I truly content with how I feel every day? Am I truly content with the direction of my life? If not, is it possible there are some things that I don't currently know about myself or about my life, or perhaps things I could do to make life better?"

I won't ever attempt to answer the first question for anyone. That one needs to be answered by each of us, as often and as honestly as possible. If the answer to the first question is not a confident YES, then I contend the second question is worth exploring further.

My answer to both questions, at least for many of my younger years was … well … I didn't ask myself those questions. I evaded these types of queries as I went down the very destructive path of addiction. When I finally did ask myself how this whole "life" thing was looking, in my late teens, the answer was, "Not so good, I think I want to change." For me, it took heading down a road that ultimately would have been a dead end, one way or the other. Either an abrupt end, due to my penchant for doing dumb things, or a slower burn dead end, where the spark of my life was slowly drained from me.

This is something for all of us to look at, and we'll talk about it further as we go. What does it take sometimes? What do we have to experience to decide to make changes? There are the flagrant trespasses against ourselves, which can be easier to see. What about the things that make our soul slowly leak from us, that we may not recognize for decades?

So many times, we're heading down a destructive path and we go on autopilot, not understanding the impact we're having on our family, friends, and co-workers. Much less, ourselves. As we move through these pages, let's ask ourselves the questions posed and do our best to pay attention to how we feel as we do.

Before we do that though, let's set up some guideposts that will help to temper our expectations. Is anyone happy, fulfilled, and content all the time? Not anyone I've known and perhaps not anyone you've known, right? If there are those people, they're probably up in the Himalayas somewhere just chilling and meditating, sipping on the occasional cup of tea. If that's what you're searching for, then this may not be the right book for you. What we'll be discussing is to be accomplished in the midst of the life we're currently living. Escaping is not a viable strategy, as it will only end in misery, confusion, internal unrest, and angst. This is not a book about waking up every day and doing just enough to exist. This book is about *living*, it's about more than we currently think is possible, especially inside us.

Feeling good about the direction of our life is something that's developed over time by paying attention to and aligning ourselves with a way of living that heretofore we may not have explored. We dive into this more deeply in a bit, but suffice it to say for now, that adopting an intentional, conscious approach to our days here, will allow us to begin to construct a thread through our life that will lead to our desired destination, as well as much more. We will begin to understand that life does not have to be a fight, if we're willing to do the work and weather the storms.

When I refer to "destination," it is important to understand that this is not actually a destination. There may never come a time when we are able to say, "Whew! I made it! Nothing else to do." In fact, it's quite the opposite. Once we start to weave the thread that leads to a more contented and fulfilling life, we'll be compelled to expand it. We'll start to wake up feeling differently; we'll start to respond to things in a different way, and some of us will even decide to see how deep the rabbit hole goes. There is no end to the exploration and subsequent bounty that can be unearthed in this lifetime, within us and outside ourselves, if that is also desired.

Please do not confuse this with putting on a happy face and forcing ourselves to be "positive" in all we say and all we do. A positive attitude and outlook isn't something we flip the switch on and pretend, once we read a book about it or see someone on SM embodying that pretense. There is something about a forced or manufactured "positive attitude" that speaks to the opposite of what it's meant to portray. It's more a sign of weakness than it is a sign of strength.

I am all in favor of looking at things positively, but that's something we earn with a lot of time and effort. We develop by adopting a way of life that supports and engenders that end. Then it comes naturally, meaning it comes from a deep, contented place and is probably not "bubbly." It's something much more convincing than that, something much more authentic. When one has a still, fulfilled heart, it's recognized because it's uncommon. It does not require moment-by-moment manufacturing.

Now, this doesn't mean that everything is bright and cheery all the time. It doesn't mean things go our way. It doesn't mean we won't be disappointed. It simply means that we can learn to approach life from a place of calm that includes an inner strength rarely seen in our world today. Is this something you want?

What might it be like to stop fighting? Have you ever pondered this? I certainly hadn't until it was brought to my attention by a mentor who was on the journey I longed to embark upon, even though I was clueless as to what it might entail.

Up until that crucial juncture in my life, I was taught to fight. I was taught to wrestle with things until I "win." I imagine you were too. Fight with problems, fight with injuries, fight beliefs different than ours, fight illness, fight enemies, fight …

That's the way to get the most out of life, right? Fight for it!

In my experience, as one who has done a lot of fighting, wrestling, trampling, and being trampled, it's not.

If I take the time to look at the payout of the fighting I've done in my life, mostly with myself, I find that I've exacerbated misery, bad habits, pain, illness, injuries, confusion, etc.

We're here to explore and uncover a better way, a more meaningful and purposeful way, which will enhance your life as well as those whose lives you touch. Isn't that what we all ultimately want anyway? To be good for ourselves and good for others?

The wonderful news is, you will find that you need not be alone on your quest. People will be attracted to that energy of authenticity and the evolution of you, discussed in this book. When you begin to change and grow past and through your previously held beliefs, attitudes, and the attendant actions, you may be surprised to find that like-minded people will show up on your journey. At the very least, you will begin to recognize people who are on a similar journey, as well as those who aren't.

Let's continue to examine how we get there.

First, I think it's important to take a look at the myriad erroneous ways that many choose to attempt to weave the threads of happiness and fulfillment into their lives.

Perhaps to this point in our life we haven't asked many questions and we've just tried to "go along to get along," thinking whatever we're doing and whatever we have planned after that, is the way. Maybe we haven't entertained the possibility of something more and we, more or less, do what everyone else does. Do we want to be crowd followers? To be accepted and part of the "in" or popular group? Do we want more than that? Everyone wants something, and it's likely that the easy path that's been presented to us every minute of every day is all we know. It's what our family does, it's what our friends do, it's what advertising and social media teach us. Do what everyone else does and you'll be happy, or at least you'll be accepted. Doesn't that sound great? Don't make any waves and be accepted by everyone.

That can and probably will work, at least for a while. It may be a reasonable strategy when we're young, when we're getting our "sea legs" under us and starting to navigate the terrain that we call the "human experience." What about when we're turning into adults? I'd have to recommend against it, but could it "work" for our entire life? Maybe, if we don't want anything more than what everyone else has and what everyone else is doing. It's a simple formula: Do what everyone else does and get the results everyone else gets. Done deal. Be born, comply, don't ask questions, rinse, repeat ad infinitum, die.

Please don't misunderstand, I'm not condemning what anyone does and how they live their lives. Many people don't want anything more than what they have and are content with where they're at. That is completely cool, and I respect what everyone is and what everyone chooses as their path. This book is not for them. I was not one of those people, and my choice early in life was a destructive path that didn't work. I was faced with no choice but to change or descend to what was likely going to be a very devastating ending, for myself and others. This book is for those to whom that little voice is speaking, telling them there's something more, and they're considering listening.

What about those who struggle with the status quo but haven't yet discovered there's a different or better way and resort to another aspect of "doing what everyone else does"? They turn to something else to nourish that desire for more and subsequently compromise themselves because they were not able to find what they desired through the original means. Let's spend a little time looking at a few of those.

With the advent of social media, many people spend their days looking for "likes" or "reactions" and base how they feel or their value in this world on how others, mostly strangers, react to them. There is really no basis in reality, as they try to put the best or funniest or most attractive version of themselves out there and get people to respond with something that makes them feel good, or at least better than they feel without that attention. The audience never sees the pain, the tears, the feelings of loneliness or emptiness. There is no authenticity with which to truly understand the purveyor.

Many turn to substances to dictate how they feel. Is that what they want? Do they want to be dependent on something other than themselves to determine how they feel or alter how they think and/or feel about their life? I'm guessing probably not. Who would consciously want to give control of their life over to a drink or a drug, prescription or otherwise, to determine how they feel? That form of "chasing happy" offers nothing but momentary reprieve. Those who continue it over a longer period find only misery, confusion, and that big hole in the middle of their chest called "unfulfilled."

What about the overuse/abuse of food, gambling, shopping, or sex? Or the myriad other distractions that can be used to help us feel differently or replace an unwanted feeling with something that for the moment is "better." Is it really "better" if we end up gambling all of our money or possessions away? Is it really better if we're constantly distracted by our desire to fulfill what we think we "need" at a heavy cost to other parts of our life? Is it really better if we end up obese or a candidate for numerous diseases because of how we've treated our body?

There are people we all know who seem to be more connected to their problems or their issues than to their desire for a life free of those burdens. Or at least free from being addicted to or dependent upon those burdens. Many don't know that they can, and are allowed, to get out of their own way to experience their lives, as opposed to just their problems.

Many are addicted to their own comfort. Their ever-shrinking emotional world has no room for the uncomfortable feelings we all experience from time to time. Now of course we all want to be comfortable to differing degrees; however, these folks shun what they deem "discomfort" at all costs. The control they attempt to exert on their outer circumstances, including the people in their lives, to achieve the demanded level of comfort, can be astounding. The tough part to watch is the more they thrash around and demand comfort, the more uncomfortable they become. It is difficult to watch, and the progression is very similar to any other addiction.

What about those to whom nothing can ever be right? You tell them they just won the lottery, and they'll figure out a way to make it a bad thing. It's almost like they're addicted to negativity, or they just can't allow themselves to be happy because it's too much of a commitment. Someone might expect something from them if they put on a smile. Is that how we go about our days? Always looking for something wrong as opposed to something right?

Is it reasonable to think that people want these things to determine how they go about their days? To determine how they feel when they wake up in the morning? To determine how they interact with others and how their relationships are ultimately shaped? I would contend that the answer to all of these questions is emphatically NO. However, that's all they currently know because it's all they've been either taught, or perhaps they've neglected, for a myriad of reasons, to learn or commit to anything different.

What if you don't fit into any of the descriptions we've discussed? What if you feel there's a better life for you out there somewhere and a better way to feel on a daily basis? What if you just can't put your finger on what's wrong, but you feel you're not performing at the level you'd like? What if your fears stop you from moving forward or taking that step? I promise you that this book is for you as well. You will never regret the adoption of a way of life based on a path that has worked for countless others. There truly exists a way to live that works, and there are innumerable ways that don't. Our decision must be whether we're willing to engage and do the work, or keep going the way we're going.

I'm reminded of a conversation I overheard recently. Two younger women, likely in their early thirties, were discussing prospects having to do with their financial wherewithal. One of the young ladies made the statement: "There is no way my generation is ever going to be able to afford to buy a home. Things are just so difficult for us. There's just no way."

You can only imagine how my heart sank, listening to this fatalistic belief system. And she believed it for an entire generation! What do we do with that? How does one overcome that? If I saw her again and I had this book in my hand, I'd just hand her a copy and say, "Perhaps there's another perspective. It won't hurt to find out, right?" as I nod and look her in the eye to try to get her to nod.

If you can relate to this or other examples or stories, you've picked up this book for a reason.

To be frank, by all the usual measurements, I probably shouldn't have what I have either. From where I started to where I am currently is quite a stretch. I guess that's the point though. If we don't stretch, we'll get what's within our reach, and that's it. If we stretch, we have a shot at things much more profound and incredible. Either we are or we're not harnessing ourselves to a preconceived life. Do we believe in a life of abundance, change, and possibility? If not, we may be destined for a life mired in self-defeat.

We're human, we all meet at a place called emotions. We all meet at a place where we desire to be liked, loved, cared for, happy, content, seen, cool, and important. I certainly did. The difference is how we get to a place where we can experience something different, something better and fulfilling.

By the time I was 14, my dad and I had long graduated to shaking hands instead of hugging, and I don't ever remember the word "love" being thrown around our house at all. We heard that word at church when we were being told how much God loves us. That was just the way it was at that time, I believe. I know my parents loved me, but that word and the attendant affection, seemingly more abundant (at least on the surface) these days, was not dripping from anyone in my family. That's okay, I have no complaints or regrets about how I was raised. It was just how it was back then in many families.

Like most kids, and in many cases, adults, I didn't know that there were things that I was going to want at some point in my life, like contentment, peace of mind, confidence, and wisdom. All I thought I wanted, and it was probably enough for me at that point, was to be liked, to have fun, to have some friends, and hopefully someday, to be cool.

It seemed the easiest and most direct way to achieve those wants at that juncture was to try to impress. How high could

I jump my motorcycle in that old gravel pit? How much beer could I drink? How much dope could I smoke? How many points could I get in that basketball game? Which dare was I willing to agree to? How could I embellish as much as possible to sound cooler than I was? I had to impress friends, and I tried to impress bosses, who at that time in my life were farmers. The way to impress them was to work as hard as possible for as long as possible and lift and carry as much as possible. It was all very exhausting, but I didn't know at that point how exhausting it would prove to be. The physical exhaustion of hard work at least has many redeeming qualities. The mental and emotional exhaustion of trying to keep up and trying to impress is a different kind of exhaustion. It's draining and has no redeeming qualities that I'm aware of. All I knew at that point in my life was that I needed to be something to the people in my life, and I thought that this was the way to do it. I didn't know any better.

Those strategies to get to what I thought I wanted seemed to work for a while. They motivated me to try very hard at things I thought mattered to my peers. I ended up in the "cool kids" category and cemented my status although there was never a feeling that I could let up on "impressing" those around me. Hence, as I had to constantly outperform my last bullshit story, drinking and drug adventure, or work escapade, I had no idea what I was doing to my body, mind, heart, or soul.

Unfortunately, the desire to impress and be all of these things did not extend to teachers, grades, parents, or responsibility, which would create its own set of problems moving forward. The intent there was to deceive as necessary (which was often), continue to pretend I was something that I wasn't, and not get caught.

Does this resonate with you? Does this sound like something you've tried? Trying to be something you're not? It's a very fatiguing way to live and ends up bearing no fruit. Why? Because it's not real. It's not where we're designed to obtain our self-worth. We're meant to achieve that within ourselves, so that we don't have to be subject to the whims of the world outside of us. We can never achieve what we desire if the only way to get there is something over which we have no control, which is other people. To round out the thought so there's no confusion as to what we have no control over, the other two elements are places and things. If we think people, places, and things are going to get us to a happy, content, and successful place in this life, I got news: Not going to happen. Many have tried, all have failed. The groundwork must start within us. The effort must be on ourselves, in the midst of whatever life we're currently living.

Let's take a moment to look at what we all want as human beings. As we start to move toward adulthood or many times deep into our adult years, there may be a realization or feeling that things aren't what we thought they were, and perhaps we aren't where we thought we'd be. Especially in how we're either approaching life or maybe just how we feel every day. Perhaps there's a specific issue and perhaps we haven't discovered anything in particular yet, but there's a feeling of unrest or discomfort with our life or ourselves. It's important to realize that we start wherever we are. We must bloom where we're planted, wherever that is. We can be in the ditch or the weeds, or maybe we're just looking for direction. It doesn't matter. If there's a crack in the veneer, no matter how slight or how big, it may be enough to embark on the journey of doing things differently.

So, what is it that most of us want as human beings on this planet?

- Happiness/contentment

- Peace of mind

- Meaning/purpose

- Good relationships

- Financial security

A reasonable list that I think everyone wants at some point in their life. The difference is probably how those wants are articulated and the avenue(s) we choose to get to a place where those wants become reality in our life. We've discussed some of the more destructive ones already, which, as we know, do not bear the promised fruit.

If we're not currently comfortable that we're experiencing these things as reality in our life, let's refer to this as a "wishlist." How does the "wishlist" resonate? How would it feel to have most, or all those things come to fruition in our life consistently? I'm sure there are some other "wishes" to add, but how would our life be if we had these things as a part of our every day? Did we know they were possible? Had we thought of life in these terms and with these things in mind? We probably don't for much of our life, especially in our youth. Many of us aren't ever introduced to anything other than what everyone else is doing, which is an easy path to follow, at least for a while. Until we ask ourselves if there is something more than what most people are doing. That little voice inside confirms that there is more, but we must put in the work to uncover it and then more work to actually live it. Living it means adopting it as a way of life.

At some point, we may find ourselves seemingly without a choice but to want things that are a little more real, as we beat ourselves up by chasing the need to impress and the need to be what we have convinced ourselves that everyone else thinks we should be. Carried through a lifetime, this will be a fatiguing, fruitless, and dead-end journey. We can never, ever achieve a contented, thoughtful, and genuinely free life when our goal is the approval of others.

It's worth noting that the list above does not mention having lots of money in the bank. There's no mention of owning a big house, expensive cars, or taking lots of vacations. All of these things are possible as well. The interesting thing to realize is that when the journey described in the coming pages is embraced and we engage in the process of working on and with ourselves first, the money can come, the big house and cars can come. If and/or when they do material-ize, they'll be included in the process of growing, learning, and implementing certain standards. To be clear, standards for us, not for others. Interestingly, if we do the work to achieve the most valuable things a person can acquire in this life such as love, humility, and unselfishness, there will be much less value placed on the items available for money. Don't get me wrong, they're nice to have, and being in a good financial position is itself a freedom. However, if that pursuit is all we cultivate and all we work for, we will likely pass up the freedom that accompanies diligent effort in other, more important facets of this life.

It's important to note here, as we begin to look at where we started, where we are currently, and where we'd like to end up someday, that a "northerly" route, intentionally aiming for what we'll call "True North" in our life, can take us to great heights within ourselves and potentially in our outer circumstances. A "southerly route," or aimless, unintentional living, feeding mostly instant gratification, can take us to places we probably don't want to go. Maybe you've already traveled a bit on the southerly route and you're seeking change, not certain where to turn. Glad you're here. This book is intended to help you.

There are also sub-trajectories in our life that feed into our overall trajectory, which we'll discuss further as we go along. Some examples of these sub-trajectories might be—how are we in our familial or spousal relationship? How are we in our business relationships? Are we fair-minded, even-handed, and supportive? How about our work ethic or our willingness and desire to move our life forward? Are we a "hand-out" type of person, or are we making our way and taking responsibility for our contributions to our community and to society?

How about as a parent? Are we cognizant of the fact that what we do bleeds into our kids, whether we like it, or agree, or not? It isn't what we say, so please abandon that thought process immediately. It's what we do. If you're showing your kids how to be angry, jealous, addicted, obese, whiny, or miserable, you're shirking your responsibility as a parent and teacher. Might suck to hear, but that doesn't make it untrue.

Teaching responsibility, kindness, forthrightness, discipline, and temperance will not only make you proud as a parent, it will also serve the most important people in that equation: your kids.

I am a stepparent. I knew one thing when my stepsons were young, as I'd been on a journey of self-improvement for about twenty years when I met Michael and Andrew. I knew that if they watched me live my life in a conscious and intentional way, it would help them with their lives. I'd have the opportunity to plant seeds that would germinate at some juncture. They may not germinate until after I'm long gone (many certainly have over the years), but that's okay. My job was to be an example, not oversee how the universe handles the boys. I know that part is above my pay grade.

There are many places in our life to improve. It's a lifelong process. That's good news, as we can continue to work and improve as long as we live. One pertinent question, if we're not happy with our trajectory, is, "If not now, when?"

I mentioned it earlier, but I'm not the one that makes the rules. I'm just here to help as many as possible understand the rules as I've experienced them, so that we can all consciously decide what we might want from the lifetime we're given.

Consequences, typically perceived as negative, are really nothing more than the result of an action, neither positive nor negative. I'm not trying to brag or anything, but I've probably made most mistakes. There was a time in my life, as mentioned previously, where I was a very active "mistake-maker," and it was abundantly apparent to many of those watching my downward spiral that I was in trouble and headed for more. Had I remained on that trajectory, the likely exit ramps would have been prison or death.

Even when I made a decision to straighten myself up, or at least put forth the effort, I made more mistakes. I continue to make mistakes, but the difference is, now I consciously endeavor to hurt no one, including myself. Intention is powerful in many ways and in so many facets of our life. Consequence is tied to intention, and when we consciously choose to do no harm, or as little as possible, positive consequences ensue. What we must remember is that we are responsible for consciously and intentionally choosing what we do and how we respond to all aspects of our life. In the following chapters, we'll explore how to do just that.

Before we embark further on this journey, in case you were wondering, to my knowledge I did not break Ted's boat. I did get invited back for several more races and continued my journey of doing interesting and in many cases, uncomfortable things. Many of which I did not, in any way, feel prepared for.

CHAPTER TWO

TRUE NORTH AND FENDER BENDERS

"I'm just not a risk-taker like you," my brother, Kevin, explained to me on yet another occasion, as I tried to pry him out of his comfort zone. I say, "yet another," because I can be quite obstinate when it comes to wanting more for those I love. It has nothing to do with Kevin, it has to do with me.

"Okay, sorry, I'll shut up," I said as I relented, recalling in somewhat fuzzy detail how many times he'd told me the same thing. I'm going to say up to ten. I guess I'm nothing, if not relentless.

The point is, not everyone is built for this book or this way of life. Now, Kevin has his own small business and enjoys freedoms that many do not, from the perspective of choosing how a living can be made. In addition, he consciously chooses not to go out of his comfort zone to do something more or different. He's not defeating himself unconsciously, which is a very different malady. He's thought about it, and he is choosing, which I certainly respect.

Meanwhile, I've been quite the opposite in terms of risk-taking and comfort zone. I've taken a lot of risks and have been out of my comfort zone the majority of my life. Is one way better than the other? No. It's a matter of preference and tolerance. The point is, are we conscious or unconscious about our choices?

If we choose to be conscious and we choose to want more from every facet of our life and desire to improve our trajectory overall, we will need to make conscious choices about how we treat every aspect of this life. Should we choose not to embark upon the journey, that's okay. I recommend to keep reading anyway, as there may be an epiphany somewhere in these pages.

Let's just say we're curious and we want to know more. Maybe we're saying to ourselves, "This whole 'trajectory' thing is intriguing, but what does it really mean and how do I alter my trajectory if that's what I decide to do?" This book was written to answer that question. Let's begin the discussion with some basics.

There are these pesky little concepts that seem to try to rear their heads in us as individuals or in society from time to time that can neither be proven nor disproven by science, but they are as true as the sky is blue for those who live by them. They can make one's day and they can wreck one's day, but those outcomes do not diminish the power these constructs can have when used either properly and regarded, or avoided and disregarded. They have the same power either way and the great news is that they can make a life productive, contented, and meaningful, or doom a life to uncertainty, selfishness, and anxiety.

They've been around since the beginning of time, and they will be around long after you and I leave this rock. They do not change based on how we humans feel, and they do not revise their impact or their gravity as we justify, blame, and try to talk our way out of adhering to their message and their validity. They were used as life-giving light by the wisest of men and women and discarded by those walking with the shadows. They cannot really be defined, but for those who live by them, there's no other way. Once you've traveled with these giants you cannot forget or discard their message, no matter how hard you try. They can boost your mood and lighten your spirit when they walk beside you, and they can poison your day and devastate your soul when you purposefully ignore them. There will never be a time when they don't matter, but in this current time many are working to abolish them, not understanding that they cannot be abolished. Technology doesn't change them in any way, and if there was ever a time when they are most applicable, it's when we believe we can outsmart them.

Do they require perfection? Do they threaten destruction if we don't dance to their tune every moment of every day? They do not. They ask that we acknowledge them and integrate them into our life to the best of our ability. They ask that when they whisper their wisdom into our heart, that we keep the signal clear by not ignoring their good judgment. If we don't keep the signal clear, we may stop hearing their message. They know that if we don't heed their often-soft voice, we may not heed when they speak in more forceful tones. At that point we may be lost, and they know that. Perhaps not lost forever but lost for a time, and that time can be very damaging. This is not what they want. They want us to be our best. Best for ourselves and useful for others. They know that if we can't be good for ourselves, we can't be good for others.

Of course, we're speaking of principles, of which there are a multitude. We'll discuss a few in upcoming pages and how they can fit into our life. One definition of principle that I like: "A fundamental truth or proposition that serves as the basis for a system of belief or behavior." I also take issue with this definition because it fails to tell the entire story.

How and who we choose to be in this world and operate our life will determine, from a trajectory perspective, how our life unfolds. It will not determine everything that happens to us, but if we allow it to affect our choices and be the basis of our decision-making, there will be a pattern that develops. That pattern will be either in a northerly, or ever-improving direction; or a southerly, or ever-worsening direction. We see it every day, perhaps in our own life but surely in the world around us. We might believe that at times, we're standing still. We're not. We're always moving in a direction and that direction is based on how we're treating our world. When people, many times unconsciously, ask me, "How's life treating you?" I'll consciously reply, whilst looking them squarely in the eye, "Life is treating me like I'm treating life." I couldn't always say that, but for many years now, I've been putting in the work to be able to, and it feels good. Best of all, it works. My hope is to get as many people to give that response as I can. Let's keep going.

I'd like to clarify and illustrate what I mean by "trajectory" here, so we're all on the same page as we deepen our understanding of where we're headed and if any changes need to be made in terms of how we're "treating life."

If you get a chance to do this today, grab a ruler and draw a straight line on a piece of blank paper, all the way across the long side of the paper. Then take a sticky note and write our "wishlist" items on it. On a counter or table, place the sticky note a foot or so away from the piece of paper and point the straight line directly at the sticky note (fig. 1). The line represents living intentionally, consciously and in alignment with the principles we'll be discussing going forward, and we'll refer to pointing directly at our "wishlist" as True North.

Now, let's put our ruler against the line again but move the upper end of the line about half-inch away from True North, and draw another line. This line should be veering away from the first line, at the top (fig. 2). What happens? We might still be catching a little bit of our sticky note or "wishlist," but we're off course. Our trajectory is wrong. What if we move the sticky note further up the True North line, but five feet from the piece of paper with the line, and we look at the trajectory of that skewed line again (fig. 3)? The line completely misses the sticky note with our "wishlist" by an even wider margin, as we remain off course. What happens if we move the sticky note to the other side of the room (fig 4)? We stay off course, and we move further and further from True North, from our "wishlist."

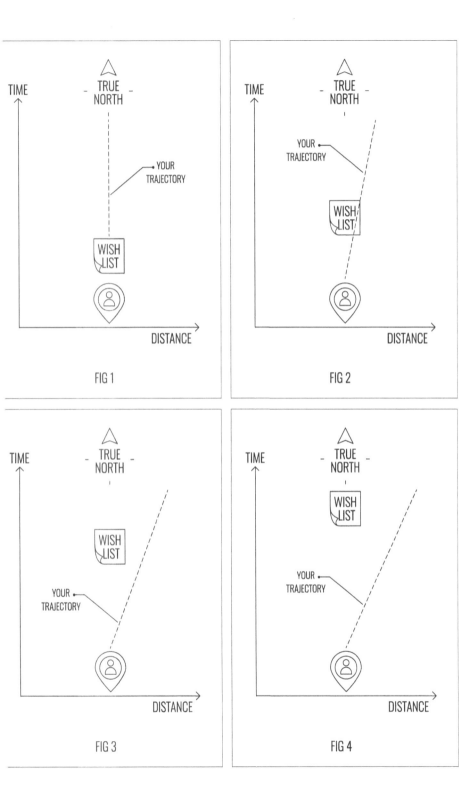

The constant is the "wishlist," which is where we also find True North. The variable is our trajectory, represented by the line as well as the amount of time we're off course, meaning how long we stay on the erroneous trajectory. It becomes apparent that the shorter time we are off course, the closer we are to our "wishlist." When the sticky note is on the other side of the room, representing a much longer period, the line that was off just a bit before, becomes way off course, perhaps to such a degree that we may decide it's not worth it to try to get back to True North. I believe this happens to a lot of us, as we go through the motions daily, as opposed to living with intention and purpose.

It becomes evident that the sooner we correct our course, the more time we have to create and enjoy a life that resonates with happiness, peace of mind, meaning, good relationships, and financial security.

There is no question that "it takes what it takes" for many of us to intentionally change course, and sometimes the commitment is stronger if we get to a point where we're "sick and tired of being sick and tired." The journey is different for everyone, and each of us must decide how far off True North we're going to allow ourselves to become.

Most of us already understand that the line is never straight and one's trajectory is imbued with twists, turns, unexpected events, stop signs, caution signs, and even a few fender benders, or worse. Perhaps another way to look at how we get from "here to there," or at least a deeper dive into understanding the journey itself, is likening it to our current way of getting to a place we don't know utilizing GPS.

We can have the best laid plans about how to get from point A to point B, including plugging the destination into the GPS. If you're anything like me, you can still get off track. Maybe we take a wrong turn; maybe we think we know better than the GPS; maybe there's unexpected traffic or road construction. Maybe someone runs a stop sign and crashes into us. All of these "life happens" moments can render our plans obsolete and cause us to go off in the wrong direction for a while, or worse, throw us off our trajectory forever. At those junctures or crossroads is where our choices lie. We're going to discuss moments of clarity as well as the awareness of crossroads we all experience in a subsequent chapter. It's important to point out now that all of us are fortunate to have moments where we know what to do and which direction to proceed. The question is, what do we choose?

Let's continue our discussion about principles and how we might begin to understand where we're headed since we now have a deeper understanding of what our trajectory can mean for our life.

What happens when we shirk honesty or unselfishness? How do things unfold for us when we fail to persevere or engage discipline or moderation as guiding principles in our life?

Failure to align our life with principle is a sure way to stifle our own reality, but it can also be incredibly taxing to the people with whom we share this existence.

Just as we can improve and evolve through an alignment, to the best of our ability, with principles, we've all seen and heard the stories of people who devolve and deteriorate based on their failure to do so. Why is that? I'd like to say again that I don't make the rules, but I've lived on both sides of principle and can report directly from the front lines that each end of the spectrum is true.

I've already chosen the southerly direction and relied upon drinking and drugs along with the attendant dishonesty, selfishness, and complete lack of discipline and moderation, and reaped the predictable reward of physical, mental, emotional, and spiritual deterioration (for my personal story, please read my first book *When I Stop Fighting*).

It was only with a rare moment of honesty at that time, that I was fortunate to see that there was another way. I was subsequently introduced to the "getting my head out of my ass" principle and began, however slowly, to adopt a different way of living. If this new way did not include adherence to a code, where previously there was none, well then, I guess it would have been a different shade of more of the same.

Over many years of doing my best and failing, or not doing my best and still failing, I guess I've had enough sprinkles of getting it right and a willingness to not give up that have helped me evolve to living the "wishlist" in my own life, for which I'm grateful. I know I can trade that in at any time and be returned to the southerly direction anytime I choose to ignore the dictums that I know to be universally true. We can adhere to and practice our life on either side of principle. It's completely up to us. We just have to know that there are rewards on either side, and the southerly trajectory will ultimately end in our defeat. This is by no means meant to be a threatening stance or intentionally fear-provoking. It's just true.

As we proceed in life, we will encounter new experiences, new obstacles, new relationships, and new paths. These will all require our attention and time. We get to decide how we're going to deploy an intentional and principle-centered way of conducting ourselves, if at all. Is it possible to get off track and then get back on? Yes, it certainly is. In fact, most of us dance to this tune our entire lives, especially if we're doing our best to live intentionally.

I was faced with this as I went from a blue-collar world to a white-collar world in my mid-to-late twenties. There were very different decisions to be made. Going from a crew of a few carpenters to dealing with companies of many more employees, many more complex interactions, and many more decisions to make, was not easy for me. I was intent on growing my life and experiencing more things, so this was the meal I was handed. Now I had to eat it.

"Daryl, did you call John yet and tell him that the client chose you instead of him?" I was asked by the owner of our company.

My head fell, "No, not yet." I was early on in business life, and at that point in my evolution, I had a very hard time giving people bad news. In this instance, I was achieving more income, which was great, but John was losing income by losing this client to me, which made me feel bad, perhaps guilty. The client asked me to tell John, so it was squarely on my shoulders to do so. No getting around it. The only way was through it, by facing it.

"Do it before you leave today," was the reply, frustration clearly seeping over the rim.

I procrastinated because I was scared. Would I have called him if I could have gotten away with not calling him? At that point in my evolution, maybe. Maybe not.

"Okay," was my reply.

A simple example but profound for me as I navigated a new avenue in life, new experience, hence new opportunity to learn how to conduct new affairs.

"Nobody ever tripped over Pikes Peak," is what comes to mind here. It's not the big things that trip us up on a daily basis. It's all the little decisions and new things we need to get good at and experience, so that we can decide how we move our life forward. The big stuff comes, without a doubt, and the big things shape us. Relationships end, people die, people betray us, etc. These big things do have an impact, for sure. More impactful, though, are the hundreds of little things that mold us and influence our trajectory. It's the decisions we make when we're faced with difficult situations. It's the choosing of options that will move us north or south, one small pact at a time.

How could not calling John have impacted me? First of all, I told the client I was going to do it. So, there's the keeping my word part. Secondly, had I not called him, there would have been this little burr in my saddle until I took care of it. I can ignore the burr, but that doesn't make it go away. Those little burrs must be addressed. If we bury them, we just accumulate garbage that must be taken out later.

I did call John that day and gave him the bad news. Another in a series of related lessons for me that had to do with an immutable and timeless fact: Just because it doesn't feel good, doesn't mean it's not the right thing to do.

I do not suffer from that issue any longer. Just in case you were wondering.

We will be faced with these lessons time and again, and they all have to do with our willingness to live in a principled fashion, or not. Sometimes we do a better job than other times and that is completely okay. Although it can be easy to beat ourselves up as we go, our focus should not be on fussily pouncing on each small instance. Our focus should be on repairing our mistakes and on our commitment to continually improve.

Is attentiveness to these quiet, patient truisms an easy way to live? No, it is not. Why? Because there is a strong likelihood that over 95% of people that are currently your family, your friends, and those whom you will inevitably encounter do not think or act in a manner consistent with the philosophies we'll be discussing in this book. Therein lies the rub, and it is difficult to overcome. It doesn't feel good to be the one who fails to follow the rest of the crowd, no matter how detrimental to us and others that blind allegiance might prove to be.

From my personal experience, I've found that perhaps following the "flavor of the day" for a while may be the catalyst for finding out what we don't want from this lifetime. Especially when we're younger and we're figuring some of these things out. As we get into adulthood though, it is incumbent on us to start to think for ourselves, explore how to grow and change, and chart our own path. Do we have the courage to be different? Do we have the fortitude to move through this life in a way that does not align with the currents of the day but does align with a principled way of living? Can we say no to the latest craze or the latest drug or the latest temptation that is not in alignment with being the best we can be? How about the pressures of business or politics or the news? If we live our life to be in concert with the tides of the day or the predilections of the moment, there is a very, very good possibility that we're on a damaging path, for ourselves and potentially others who our life may touch.

There are many reasons why we may be out of alignment with or not connecting to those forces that will allow us to experience our "wishlist." Many, if not most, are out of our control. I harken back to the "nouns" from my first book,

When I Stop Fighting. If our focal point is to control or change the people, places, and things that surround us, we're in for a rough ride. As we begin to turn the focus inward, our "wishlist" comes into view. The longer we do that, the clearer our view becomes.

Things change in the world and many of the changes are not conducive to growth, human interaction, or our best and highest good. It's not our doing or our fault necessarily, that human-to-human interaction has been interrupted by technology, right? It is not our fault that video chats have replaced in-person interaction or that we text or message instead of call. What about getting "likes" as a replacement for actual hugs? Not our fault either.

The good news is, living a new way of life in the northerly direction does not care, frankly, what's happening around us. There's an old saying, "The circumstances don't make the person, they reveal them [us] to themselves [ourselves]." There's nothing we can do about the tides of the world or the tides of our job or what our friends or family choose. Those do not dictate us, and they do not dictate which trajectory we choose. These are the choices we need to make for ourselves.

Above all, we're not here to assign or spend any time on blame, finger pointing, or victimhood. These thoughtless and time-wasting activities are for those who choose a path of detriment to themselves and others, not a path toward the "wishlist" or a contented and useful life. In the interest of clarity, when I use the word "useful," I don't mean it in a demeaning way or a way that implies that some people aren't useful. Remember, this is about you and your journey. "Useful" could mean not fighting—not fighting yourself, others, or the world—like you used to; maybe supporting your family, financially or otherwise; perhaps working to feel better about yourself and your life, so you don't drag other people down. Maybe it means not blaming circumstances outside of yourself for how your life unfolds, as explored in this chapter.

It is without dispute that a deterioration in human contact has consequences, and none of them is positive. Well, if none of these things is our fault, then what can be done? We are embarking on this journey to find that out.

What else might stand in the way of getting to the "wishlist"? There are addictions, instant gratification, wanting something for nothing, looking for the easy path instead of the path that might require courage, faith, or perseverance. Maybe we just think we're different and that the rules don't apply to us. There are endless reasons or, to be more direct, justifications as to why many of us don't reach the breadth and depth within ourselves we're designed to reach.

What would happen if we drew a line through the trajectory of our life at this moment, through all the beliefs, behaviors, attitudes, work ethic, etc., that we have recently or perhaps for many years carried with us? Where would that path be taking us in five years? How about twenty years? Does it feel good to chart that trajectory? Does it make us pause just a bit and consider what we're doing and where that track will end up? If so, that's great. We all deserve to take the time to question ourselves and why we do the things we do. Why we believe what we believe. Why we hang around and spend time with those we do. Are the things we're doing serving to enhance our life and the lives of those around us, or is it all just habit and comfort and trying not to be too inconvenienced, scared, or exhausted? Good questions to ask ourselves as we travel around in this flesh outfit.

Perhaps at this moment, we're asking ourselves, "Why would I need to change?" Well, perhaps there are consequences to how you're currently living that you may not have been completely honest with yourself about. How about things like fears that hold you back, lack of focus, lots of things you know you need to do that you don't handle, as the years tick by. What about brain fog, lost money, obesity, feeling like a lost soul? Let's look at our "wishlist" and determine whether or not we're heading toward True North. What does our trajectory look like right this moment? Is there a burr in our saddle, something we need to address? Is there something nagging us about how we live or what we do every day? Is there a change we could make right now?

As life can be fluid and ever-evolving, I purposely refrain from discussing certain step-by-step instructions for this journey. I've found it better suited to a diverse and eclectic audience to rely on examining universal laws or principles. I'm not familiar with the circumstances or varying degrees of growth anyone might be in the beginning, middle, or end of experiencing. To attempt to line up a this-then-that-then-that path, to me, could be ill-fitting and counter-productive. We'll all grow and change at a pace different from others, which leaves the decision we need to make about whether we'd like to adhere to a particular trajectory. My great hope is that decision is an emphatic, "To True North we go!" Well, fasten your seatbelt because it can be a bumpy ride, full of potholes. Not to mention, no matter how long we go or how far we drive, we'll never get there. I say that somewhat in jest but also to set the proper expectation. Just because we'll never get to True North, or "perfection," doesn't mean we shouldn't try to point our ship as close to that direction as we can.

It takes time to sort through these things and determine where we are and where we're going. Just to recognize and admit that what we currently believe is likely something passed down to us by parents, socialization, or perhaps certain events we've encountered or lived through is a solid first step. These things can affect us to the core. The big question to ask: Are these handed-down systems and beliefs working for me? Is it working for the people from whom I've inherited these beliefs and ways of doing things? Are they content? Are they living the life I want to emulate? Is their way of living going to get me to the "wishlist"? Is it getting them to the "wishlist"?

A life that is not intimidating, stressful, or constantly strenuous takes time, effort, and patience. Remember, we've been taught to fight. We've learned that we must protest, struggle, resist, and clash! It will take a concerted effort on our part to unravel this messaging and these instructions, within ourselves.

Experience will be the teacher, and it will be up to us to learn. Life will hand us the lessons and will leave it up to us as to how to move forward. There will always be difficult times and situations. We will never be able to avert or avoid those grueling occurrences as long as we live. In fact, life will get more difficult as we get older. People will let us down, leave us, and inevitably die. It's all a part of this life. If we shrink from these tough times or otherwise attempt to numb ourselves to feeling all that life will throw at us, we invite a featureless, anesthetized existence that offers no reward.

It is okay to experience difficulty, anxiety, and trying times. They are not to be run from or blunted in some way. They are meant to be felt, experienced, and moved through. These experiences show us how to be better and more durable the next time. We are not expected to exhibit the wisdom and maturity at twenty or twenty-five years old that we should certainly be at least beginning to exhibit by thirty-five or forty. It takes time, it takes experience, it takes conscious decisions on our part along the entire journey.

For now, the commitment is to make ourselves aware and take a peek behind the curtain of what we do every day and how that relates to our trajectory. Start to get a glimpse, which can be an early step toward real change. Let's keep going.

CHAPTER THREE

WHERE THE HELL'S THE DIRECTIONS?

Nobody ever taught me about this stuff when I was young, at least that I recall. We are not given a handbook. All we're given is the best our parent or parents could do at that time in their lives, which may not be helpful from the perspective of body, mind, heart, and soul. We got the best they had at that time, and maybe it didn't include many of the concepts and principles we'll be discussing in this book. That's okay, I don't mention this in order to point a finger or to blame anyone. I mention it because it's important to know where we're starting, in addition to where we want to go. There are times when our rearing shows us what we don't want or what we don't want to be or become, which can be very valuable. It can also illuminate that we might want to pick a few good things and set other things aside. It's all valuable if we set aside any blame and just look at what we might learn from those experiences.

We all get off track sometimes. It's just a part of life. Everyone gets scared, anxious, sad, lonely, lost, etc. The trick of this life is, what are we doing with this information that we don't like? What are we doing with this experience that doesn't feel good? Are we shrinking, or are we understanding that this experience or the feelings associated with it are temporary? In those moments are we calmed by knowing that "this too shall pass"? Or are we going down the path of "why me?" or "poor me," feeling sorry for ourselves?

I heard a long time ago when I was in a tough spot, "Pain is inevitable, suffering is optional." It makes an incredible amount of sense and helps me truly understand that what I do when things get difficult will truly shape me and the next tough experience that I'm destined to have. Are we looking to principle and truth to help us work through whatever pain we're encountering, or are we leaning into self-pity, assigning blame, and then smoking a joint to feel better? In my experience, the latter is the suffering part; the latter is my reaction to something I don't want to feel, and I am doing everything I can to run from it. How could running from things we don't want to feel be the winning strategy? It's not. Running only serves to ensure the next time we run into a difficult experience or feeling, it will be even more challenging because we didn't learn anything the last time. To clarify, the "joint" can be whatever we use to evade or avoid feeling something we don't want to feel. The "joint" could be drinking, other drugs, sex, food, complaining, self-pity … whatever. It could be anything that replaces the sensation that we don't want to experience.

With this in mind, how do we know whether or not we're moving in the right direction or a direction that will only serve to exacerbate our issues? I am a firm believer we all know which direction we're headed inherently because that little voice inside lets us know. That little voice gives us all the clues we need. Are we listening? Are we making progress? What is our trajectory? When we begin listening to that voice and start to experience arduous times in a different way, not running, not replacing, not evading, our life will start to change immediately. When we tell ourselves the truth and live in a way that venerates the truth at any given moment, we have changed our trajectory, we have changed the remainder of our life forever, as well as the lives of those around us. First, we must recognize when we are off the path, perhaps in the woods or the weeds and we don't even know it. Remember, what we've learned in our life if we haven't purposefully pursued our own path is whatever everyone in our circle has taught us, including family, friends, co-workers and, in many instances, strangers. In the age of social media, constant advertising, influencers, etc., strangers have a great impact on us and zero vested interest in how our life is unfolding, now or at any future time.

"Holy shit, what just happened?" I belted out as my buddy and I came to rest in a ditch near the local A&W.

He looked at me, wondering the same thing, his eyes glazed and a look of terror on his face.

"F*ck, I don't know," he said as we both noticed at the same moment that we were facing in the opposite direction of where we'd been headed.

It was the first time I'd driven that red Chevy pick-up with a gravity box full of grain behind it. I wasn't smart enough at that point to realize that the gravity box, fully loaded, was a lot heavier than that farm pick-up. So, when I needed to brake, heading down that hill toward town, the one thing I couldn't do was try to stop too fast. Unfortunately, that's what I attempted to do.

Apparently, when you do that, the much heavier object pushes that lighter object, regardless of the application of brakes, and when you hit the brakes too hard, you start to spin around in the road, prior to being deposited in a ditch. I succeeded in doing the one thing I couldn't do.

Could have been a lot worse than it was, so I was very happy that no one was hurt. A little ding on the boss's truck and some local farmers having to drag us out of the ditch.

"Keep it between the ditches," was a favorite phrase some of my friends and I shared when we were young. Out in the country in Michigan, there were generally ditches on either side of most roads and we'd end up in them from time to time, for a multitude of reasons, like the example above.

"Ha ha, okay, we'll try," was a normal reply, as there were various potential obstacles to contend with such as winter, tractors, deer, bald tires, escaped farm animals, general idiot behavior, and the substances with which we may or may not be imbued, at any given time.

Same goes for this life journey and how our trajectory fits into the story. There are problems, obstacles, and issues we may at any time be presented with. The bad news is, we will always be contending with things beyond our control, no matter which direction our trajectory is currently headed. The good news is, as we consciously decide on which direction we'd like to go, we can be the catalyst for removing ourselves from hastening the journey in a southerly direction.

Are there things we can't do, kinda like applying the brakes too fervently with a heavier load behind us? There are, and we'll be presented with the accompanying lessons as we go. Perhaps sometimes we'll just be spinning around in the road for a bit before we come to rest. Many times, we'll end up in the ditch, which isn't the worst place to be. The hope is always that there isn't too much damage as we learn our lessons.

What are some signs that our trajectory is not moving in an encouraging direction? After we discuss this, we'll start to move on to how we improve. Why does all this matter? Well, because there's going to be a quiz entitled, "The Rest of Your Life," so it's in our best interest to open up and be honest here:

- We often feel as though we have a hole in the middle of us that can't be satisfied or filled. Perhaps we can fill it temporarily with some exciting news or event in our life, but at our core we are not truly fulfilled, content, or at peace.

- We are absolutely sure about what everyone else needs to do to improve themselves. This is a very clear indicator that we are lacking the required humility to learn. Even if we are doing well in certain areas of life, there is a very real possibility (actually, a certainty) that we don't know what is right for others or their lives. The very nature of convincing ourselves that we do know is a clear indicator that we are not spending enough time on ourselves. The wisest people you've ever met are not convinced they know what's best for everyone else. This is why they're wise.

- We don't sleep well because our mind won't slow down, and we constantly worry about things that are out of our control. This happens to everyone from time to time, but as a rule, we should be settled and able to sleep well almost every night.

- We have a difficult time being alone and require constant attention or the presence of others.

- We have a difficult time being around others due to our insecurities.

- We think that someone or something outside ourselves is responsible for how we feel. This can be friends, family, bosses, strangers, government, politics, etc. "If only 'they' would change [or not do or say this or that], my life would be better."

- We believe we're owed something. Doesn't matter who we think owes us, the very nature of feeling as though we're "owed" does not leave room for our own responsibility to better ourselves.

- We want things but are not willing to put in the required work to achieve those things. We believe somehow that life is supposed to give us what we desire without the attendant effort on our part.

- We use drugs (prescription or otherwise), alcohol, food, shopping, sex, etc., to alter how we feel. The redefining of the word addiction to "therapeutic" is especially concerning as it offers justification while exacerbating the problem(s). The question to ourselves could be, "Is my 'therapy' healing me or is it just prolonging my unwillingness to face and address my underlying issues?" If what we're using as "therapy" is not currently healing us or moving us in that direction, it's not therapeutic. It's just another replacement for what we don't want to feel or face. Of course, we understand that many drugs are therapeutic or pain relieving, and have a reasonable and useful place in society. Let's not confuse those with the daily or oft daily ingestion of substances justified as "therapeutic."

- We're often full of anxiety and rarely, if ever, feel settled.

- We shrink or get uncomfortable when someone asks us if we're happy. We answer yes but know in our hearts that it's not true.

- We feel compelled to let others know how "confident" or accomplished we think we are by accumulating stuff or "knowing" things.

- We spend our days dealing predominately with and talking about our "problems" or our "ailments" without doing much to alleviate them or our attitude about them.

- We are addicted to our own comfort and cannot handle discomfort or inconvenience.

In laying these things out for us to look at, there is no determination of good versus bad or right versus wrong. These things that may or may not be applicable to us are just what they are, at this juncture in our evolution. This may just be where we find ourselves. The great news is, if we recognize some of these as pertaining to us, then we are truly beginning to "find" ourselves. That is the genesis of change and is to be celebrated. It may not feel so great as we examine what we might call our failings, but there is no other place to start. We cannot ever start if we don't first recognize that there is something that needs to change.

We must remember that there are many facets to us and how we interact and relate to others and to the world. We have a body, mind, heart, and spirit, and each of these aspects of our total being requires attention and practice, in order to reap the full benefit of our time and experience. We can be attending to certain aspects of ourselves and avoiding others. I've personally had the experience of doing well in some respects but at the expense of some, requiring me to shift my attention and address an area that I may have been ignoring. As we move our life forward, it is important to recognize where we might need additional attention and embark upon the journey of giving that awareness and consideration to all the elements that make up our being. What if:

- We're physically in shape but have a hole in our heart the size of Crater Lake?

- We're well read and "educated" but out of shape and ill in our body?

- We have financial success but no healthy relationships?

- We've convinced ourselves we're a teacher when we really need to be a student?

- We have a great work ethic but don't know how to

slow down and be grateful?

- We're "smart," but we won't answer the call to heal ourselves?

- We keep getting the same lesson presented to us, without changing our behavior or attitude?

Every facet of ourselves and how we're growing and maturing in each will contribute to who we are and how we experience the world. Body, mind, heart, and spirit work best in synergy with each other if we put effort into each one. Every aspect of us needs nourishment and attention, and it is our responsibility to find out how to do that. We weren't given a handbook. It is incumbent on each of us to build our own. I am attempting with this book to offer some clues, but I would also highly encourage curiosity, exploration, and openness to change and growth. Once those efforts are exerted, life swoops in to assist. Once we garner and use the gifts we've been given to encourage ourselves and learn and move forward, it's amazing how we are supported by forces unseen.

There are times when a breakdown of the mechanism is the only thing that gets our attention. The hope is always that the damage is not too severe. That has been what gets my attention historically, and the last almost 40 years I've spent paying closer attention and recognizing where I might be off base before there's a severe issue. In addition to that, I consistently practice the methods I've learned over time to be at my best.

"Well, my diet has not been as regimented and I've been eating some things I normally wouldn't," I explained to the functional doc, as we discussed my recurrence of IBD.

"What else have you not been doing that you know you need to do?" the doc queried.

"I haven't been consistently meditating, either," I confessed.

"I think you know what to do, Daryl. You've done it before."

"You're right, Doc. I do."

As I left the doc's office, I mumbled to myself under my breath, "You can be a real dumb ass sometimes, Daryl."

I knew what to do and I just wasn't doing it. This to me illustrates perfectly the following important teaching moments:

1. *The crucial relationship between body, mind, heart, and soul.* My body suffered because I wasn't taking care of the rest of me. I wasn't eating the diet that I knew worked to keep me symptom-free (body). If I know what the right thing to do is and I don't do

it, that little burr in my saddle, discussed previously, shows up until I get back on track and remedy my behavior (heart). I lost the mental toughness that keeps me on track by unconsciously engaging in destructive behaviors, as opposed to consciously not engaging in them (mind). I chose to shelve the discipline of meditating consistently, every day (soul). Meditation is very healing for the body, mind, and heart.

2. *The importance of choosing a trajectory in all areas of life, developing the disciplines, and executing the disciplines, consistently, over time.* There is always a cost and many times the cost is to our entire being, not just what we see, which is our body. As we progress, we can choose to expand our disciplines, but there are basic building blocks that are very necessary for us to stay on track.

3. *As illustrated to me again, the choice is always to do the work or not to do the work.* "The work" meaning what I know I need to do to either start, continue, or start over. After some experience with living intentionally and consciously, it becomes much easier to jokingly call myself a "dumb ass," as opposed to the alternative, which is beating up and chastising

myself. This is absolutely progress, as it's very easy to spend time with fruitless endeavors like self-pity or blame, as opposed to the work.

Then there are the darker alternatives. I could have chosen to continue on the path inconsistent with being healthy in body, mind, heart, and soul. What happens then?

Well, for me, as the path has narrowed, so have the bumper guards that keep me on the path. That time I hurdled them and set off on a path that I knew was inconsistent with my overall health and a northerly trajectory. I found out what happens.

People who know me know I'm sober and have been for a long time. They would probably see nothing awry with the setback I've been describing. Did I drink or do drugs? No. Did I turn back into the liar, thief, and cheat of my younger years? No. Was I being dishonest or damaging to the people in my life? No.

However, I was being dishonest with myself and treating myself poorly in a few areas. The road narrows. What I've moved past in my life will cause me pain if I go back to those behaviors, even if it doesn't appear to anyone else that I've breached the "big stuff." The small stuff becomes the big stuff at some point as we progress. I can't get away with much anymore, and I've learned that I don't want to.

The choice is always ours. First, do we want to change ourselves and progress? Second, are we ready to commit to continuing that journey, wherever it leads?

CHAPTER FOUR

THE DUMB-ASS CHRONICLES

There is no substitute for being honest with ourselves. We hear people speak about honesty, and it's very easy to cast honesty off as not telling a lie, meaning honesty with others. That's true and that is honesty, although at a very basic level. We all learned this at a very young age, whether by being instructed as to the basic tenets of living successfully with others on this planet, or by telling a lie and feeling the lesson on our backsides, or perhaps these days, being put in timeout. My experience was not the timeout. The lesson on my backside seemed to drive the message home and help me understand through experience. At least that elementary understanding of honesty. Suffice it to say that we might carry the same understanding of "honest" into adulthood that we carried when we were very young. Are there other ways to understand the concept of "being honest"?

As we've touched on, there are many facets of "us" and many ways for us to experience this life. My body (physical self) can experience relative good health, and I can run and lift weights till the cows come home, but if I don't spend time on my heart (emotional state) or soul (quiet and gratitude), they suffer and can be caught in a state of imbalance or disarray. Let me give you some other examples: If you look good, but you're miserable, what's the point? Your heart may be kind and loving and open, but why do you keep putting yourself in a bad position with the wrong people in your life? Maybe your mind, or mental toughness, needs attention. You spend significant time at church, but you're obese and often angry and impatient. You wonder what's wrong. You've mastered making money, but you feel there's a hole in the middle of your chest that never seems to go away.

Each of these aspects of ourselves is interconnected and each helps feed the others. It's much easier to be calm and still in my heart and soul when my mind and body are strong and attended to. My mind isn't as strong as it could be if my body isn't attended to in a way that supports physical health.

It's our responsibility to understand and attend to ourselves in every aspect of ourselves. That is the level of honesty we're talking about. Getting to know ourselves to such a degree that we do what it takes to understand and nourish every aspect of ourselves to the best of our ability. Internalizing and understanding in the deepest recesses of our being that we cannot get away with being dishonest with ourselves, whether we want to or not. No matter how hard we try. It's not whether anyone else finds out or even if we find out; it's that we already know, despite what we might try to tell ourselves. If we're miserable while trying to act like we're not to everyone else, we're lying to ourselves. If we spend all of our time being financially successful and hide behind our expensive toys and cars and homes and can only sleep two hours per night because we can't slow our brain down, perhaps we're not as successful as we think. How about if we overeat to the point of obesity but try to act like we eat healthily when others are around? Maybe we use substances to stem the emotions we don't care to feel because of our very stressful job helping others recover from addictions.

Congruence is crucial, to reap as much benefit as well as synchronicity between body, mind, heart, and soul. If we're doing our best to treat all these aspects of ourselves with respect and attention, we're amplifying our message to ourselves and leaving less room for internal turmoil. If we're ignoring aspects of ourselves, we're disconnecting important pieces of ourselves that could be contributing to our highest good. Incongruence, or ignoring our responsibility to tend to all of ourselves, leads to deterioration over time. There's always a cost. The cost of doing the right things for ourselves is time, energy, and the necessary amount of effort. The cost of ignoring all or a part of ourselves that requires attention is, or can be addictions, phobias, fears, illness, distance from ourselves, distance from others.

If we stop long enough, pay attention, and get honest for even a short time, we can see how these choices continuously play out in our life. To use that information to shift our life strategy and explore ways to improve based on even a brief illumination is the beginning of utilizing the innate wisdom that's in each one of us. Sometimes all it takes is a few moments of clarity and honesty to turn our trajectory in a different direction.

There are an infinite number of ways to justify to ourselves the behaviors we might engage in that should be serving to illuminate us to … ourselves. That's where honesty comes in and that's where, if we're truly going to make progress in all our indispensable realms, we need to seek more balance of attention to each, hence achieve more balance in our life, as a result.

We must ask ourselves the crucial questions, like those above, and then be honest about the answers. Maybe we have an over reliance on work or weed or food or drinking or exercise. Maybe we've spent zero time in the gym or all our time in the gym. Maybe we meditate for seven hours a day but can't pay the rent. Who knows? It's for each of us to determine for ourselves and is the starting point for the journey to feeling better and being better than we were yesterday.

What am I allowing myself to do and why? What do I think I'm getting away with that I now know I'm not getting away with? Is what I'm doing every day moving me in the direction I want to go? Remember when we drew the line through our trajectory to determine where we're headed—how do things look five years from now? Twenty years from now? Time to be completely honest.

We're "earning" wherever we are in this life. Maybe not on a moment-to-moment basis but as it pertains to our trajectory. It's imperative to ask ourselves the questions and then answer honestly. What am I allowing myself to do? Are these things moving me in the direction I'd like to go or just satisfying momentary desires? Is that cake so damn tasty that I can't say no? Am I so upset about work that the only way I've found to deal with it is to drink or smoke a joint? Where are those "remedies" taking me? What am I doing to "earn" where I am, not to mention, where I'm headed?

If we haven't realized it yet, it's time to realize that nobody is going to do this life for us and nobody is going to reap either the detriment or the benefit of our decisions and behaviors except us. Sure, we'll affect people along the way, but if we choose to affect them in a respectful, helpful way, it also affects us; and if we choose to be demanding, demeaning, and closed, that also goes into our trajectory.

How are our relationships? When we're young, it makes sense that we want as many friends as possible and as many people as possible to like us. I get it. Been there, done that. As we move along and mature into our life, the value of each human being should increase, especially those closest to us. No matter how our life stacks up—big family, small family, no family—this is a starting point for most of us and we're blessed if we have at least some of these people in our life. How are those relationships? Am I contributing to better relationships in my family or am I not? Am I a good daughter, son, sibling, parent, or partner? Am I supportive of others or just concerned with myself?

I understand that families can be intricate and interesting relationships. I also absolutely understand that there are many people in life who bring toxicity, and many times those people can be members of our family. Not only are they toxic to themselves but also to others, especially their family.

There are a lot of takers out there and certainly less givers. Just because someone is a member of our family does not mean that they are solid people for our life. I've found that I can love a family member but also not allow that family member to affect my life in a negative way. This is imperative to understand so that we don't get caught up in the web of noxious behaviors that can accompany familial relationships. We can also embrace and be grateful for those family members that support us and cherish our journey as well as their own.

"Look, I'll lend you the money, but when you get your large payment, I need your assurance that you'll pay me back."

"Oh, yes, of course! I appreciate your help so much! I'll definitely pay you back."

Unbeknownst to the party in question, this was merely a test. I don't need the money and I never expected to get it back. I was, however, testing to see if the proclaimed "I'm doing my best to be a better person" declarations were true.

This family member has a history of taking advantage of almost everyone who has come into her life, including her parents. For whatever reason, she became and remained incredibly self-absorbed and toxic to those whose lives she touched.

I had loaned her money several other times and always received the promise that it would be paid back. Never a dime.

This time I decided it would be different. In addition to the money this time, I also spent several hundred hours navigating and negotiating some items for her that she was neither comfortable nor fit to handle.

"Just let me know when that large payment comes in, okay?"

"Oh, I will. I get so stressed out about paying you back. I'll be glad when I can."

I almost had to laugh at this point as it had gotten to the point of ridiculous.

I haven't heard a peep since, and it's been years. I know she received the large payment as well, which I'm sure is why I haven't received any communication.

Why do I bring up this story? Because it doesn't matter if it's a family member or not. Toxic people are toxic people, and we should do all we can to keep them at a safe distance from our peace of mind and serenity.

The other important point to bring up is how important it is to keep our side of the street clean. I knew what I was getting into, and I knew the likely conclusion. I had a long history of helping this person through numerous problems, issues, and difficult circumstances, with no thought of getting any-thing in return. I probably went way past what I should have done to be helpful.

I needed to convince myself that I had done all I could do and had to feel like I wasn't leaving anything on the table, in terms of what I could do to try to help. I didn't leave any-thing on the table, and now I'm just done. It feels good to be done sometimes, especially when you know you've done your best.

One last point. It's important, along with and as a part of being done, that no ill will be harbored. I do not dislike this family member, nor do I wish her any ill will. She must live the life she lives, and I've just chosen to not be a part of it. I've also chosen not to attempt to explain to her what she already knows.

What about friends? Do your friends number in the hundreds or thousands and include people on social media that you've never met? How many close relationships do you have where you'd do anything for them, and they'd do anything for you at a moment's notice? I'd have to guess that number is less than five. These are probably the ones that, as we get old-er, we'll cherish more and more. They don't have to be the ones where every value aligns, but I'd bet that there's an unbreakable code there that is shared and highly valued.

It's important to understand who our most treasured friends are, because when we're young, we don't yet realize how many people will come into and out of our life. Especially in the age of social media. There will be a lot of posers and very few of the priceless friends. It's crucial to flag the quality relationships and nurture those as long as we can, hopefully forever.

Are our intimate relationships characterized by something other than shared values, shared commitment, and shared responsibilities? Am I a lost puppy looking for someone to take care of me, or am I the lost puppy "whisperer," so that I can feel good about trying to fix someone else, so I don't have to pay attention to all my defects? We've all been there, perhaps more than once. Am I growing enough in my own life to recognize this in my relationships? Or do I numb what's going on with other distractions that keep me from taking a good, honest look at my relationships?

These are difficult questions to answer, and all require a level of honesty that heretofore we may not have gifted ourselves. It sucks to illuminate these things, but it's the only way to effect real change. It's the only way to get started on the real journey, the journey that may include reversing or revising a course that's leading away from our "wishlist."

I can attest that mistakes are just another part of the journey. I'm pretty sure I've made most of them. The more I've made, the more lessons I've been presented with. That's not permission to do dumb shit, but it is an acknowledgement that if we do make mistakes, it's okay. Not only is it okay, but it's also inevitable. A very important part of our journey is to learn to accept that we will make mistakes and start to be able to recognize that little voice that's directing us when we're about to make one. Do we listen, or do we execute the dumb shit anyway? This takes time and it takes patience with ourselves. As we learn to lean away from doing the things that the little voice is telling us not to do, we'll be able to avoid a lot of the trouble we might have gotten into.

"As long as I keep up the ibuprofen and the icing, I should be okay for Sunday," I told my teammates, as I limped off the basketball court.

My knees were killing me, especially the right one. I didn't know it then, but I'd torn my ACL a little over ten years before, playing wallyball soon after getting out of college, and my unstable knee was being shredded ever since. Never went to the doc for it. That's what ACE bandages are for anyway, right?

I'd had three meniscus repair surgeries at that point, and the deterioration was abundantly evident. As had been my way,

I continued to play, and at that time, I was 35 and still playing in four very competitive leagues, as well as pick-up ball when I could. Lots of ice, lots of ibuprofen.

Basketball was my drug at that point in my life, and I'd never entertained not playing. It was my competitive outlet, and I was pretty good, so a lot of guys would ask me to play on their teams.

The following Sunday came. I was in the game, hurting no more than usual, when I jumped to try to block a shot and I felt my knee come apart. That's the only way I know how to describe it … come apart.

"You okay, D?" I was asked, as I hobbled back and forth down the court, trying to "shake it off."

"I don't think so," was my half-heartedly hopeful and at the same time pissed-off reply.

I'd had worse pain and was not one to show pain or let it stop me, which was why I was in this situation in the first place.

"So, not great news, Daryl," the surgeon explained. "To put it bluntly, your knee was developing bone on either side to try to fuse itself together, due to the instability over so many years. By the way, I don't see an ACL in there anywhere."

"Well, that sucks, I guess."

"You have the knee of an 80-year-old. I can stabilize it with a new ACL, but if you keep playing, you're going to need a knee replacement by the time you're forty."

I must admit, I wasn't too surprised. I quit playing basketball that very day. Another lesson to log in the dumb-ass chronicles, of which I've had many.

Same mistake(s) over and over again? Not being honest with myself, over and over again? Not asking for help, over and over again? Lots of juicy lessons in there.

One other thing about mistakes that we touched on briefly a bit earlier: We don't do well when we continue to consciously make the same mistake(s). "I didn't mean to" only works so many times. When someone says that to us, sometimes it's appropriate to ask, "But did you mean not to?" We can't let ourselves off the hook so easily if we're serious about moving forward on this journey. Taking responsibility and changing our trajectory means that before the mistake, we ask ourselves honestly, "What could be the consequences here? What happens if I do this in a different way? Or not at all?"

A big part of being authentic and candid with ourselves is coming to the point where we can admit and accept that we need help. Help with what? Help with whatever is keeping the old way of doing things intact and keeping a new way of doing things from blossoming in our life. The only way to have a different life is to do things differently. I have never been one to easily concede that I need help, but when it comes to making big changes in life, we must acknowledge that we all do, which I've gotten much better at over time. Here's where some humility comes in. Not humiliation, humility. An indispensable part of changing the direction of my path is to acknowledge that I need help and then be humble enough to accept it. Humble is another word for "teachable," and changing up the trajectory of the journey requires being teachable. Am I ready to admit I need help? Am I ready to accept help? Can I set aside what I think I know (which coincidentally (or not) has brought me to the place where I need help)?

When difficult things happen, it's easier to take stock of where we're at. Those junctures can illuminate where we've been off, maybe for years, perhaps decades. My knee story is a perfect example. I needed to open myself to other ways to live, other avenues to explore, and different ways of doing things. What else is out there for us? Many times, it's difficult to see out of the hole to which we've grown accustomed. But it's peering through the pain that can be illuminating; it's the difficulty that spurs us to lift our head and look outside the hole to a larger landscape. The more we do this, the more expansive the landscape becomes until finally, we peer out of the hole and begin to understand that the universe(s) available to us is far beyond our wildest imagination. When we realize and internalize this, we can leave the hole for good.

Keeping our eyes on the prize, one day at a time, is vital as we begin to admit and accept that what we've been doing is no longer working. Why? Because it is not easy to change. It is not easy to accept that we must change if we want a different life, but then embarking on the journey can be overwhelming, uncomfortable, and confusing.

"Pain is the only instrument sharp enough,

to prune away the excesses of our wayward will,

and shape it into some reasonable facsimile,

of [the Universe's] will for us."

—*Acceptance*

Why is it so difficult for us to foment change without some sort of pain? Why does it usually take anguish for us to want to change? I wish I knew. My body would be a lot more intact, that's for sure, if I'd listened to what it was telling me for years, before some parts finally gave up and broke down, piece by piece.

Emotional and mental anguish can be even worse. What about staying in relationships long past their "use by" dates? How about jobs where we hang in there for 40 years come hell or high water, ignoring our misery? What about the people we allow to influence us long after we know the destruction they can wreak on us and our life?

In many instances I'd have to say that, as much as it hurts, thank God pain pushes us in certain directions. What if it didn't? What if we stayed in ruinous situations our entire life? What if nothing ever spurred us to seek a different way or a different path?

The universe gives us an opportunity through and because of adversity. Some never heed the call, which is quite sad to watch. Many times, these people can be our family members and friends, which makes it more difficult to witness. Some do, and it's an occasion for celebration.

Unfortunately, there's no magic pill. The good news is, as we embark upon a journey of change, we find that the journey itself can be rewarding, and if we stay on it long enough, it becomes indispensable as food, water, or oxygen. Maybe more so. We will find that if we exert ourselves, commit to a new path, and stay on that path as it twists, turns, upsets us, helps us, hurts us, and ultimately transforms us, we will end up grateful for every step along the way. The effort and the struggle are what bring us from stuck to progressing; unconscious to aware; thankless to grateful.

Since we're being honest here, we must ask ourselves, "What are the alternatives if I choose not to improve? Where am I going from here if I choose to stay on the same path?" Tough questions, but nonetheless necessary. Wouldn't it be nice if we could all just go along with destructive behaviors, limiting and self-defeating beliefs and be magically healed every month or so? We could do all the damage we wanted because we knew that there was a magic pill we could take and be all better whenever we wanted to be. Then, once we're healed, we could start all over on the path of ruination. The bad news is, there's no such pill. The good and better news is, there's no such pill. There are, though, ways we can move past and beyond anything that is stopping us.

Many years ago, I was presented with the prospect that addiction is a disease, and that addicted people are just suffering from an ailment, much like cancer or an autoimmune disorder. There's another school of thought that believes addiction is a malady of the spirit.

I would have to say that I'm probably somewhere in the middle of these perceptions. I found it easier once I started on a path of sobriety, as some of the fog cleared (not to mention, my head began to come out of my ass), to discard any label and place my focus on what I needed to do to get better. I began to believe that in the final analysis, it's up to me to get past my addiction(s). If I choose to call addiction a disease, then I think I'd have the best disease ever created because it's one that I have the power and the responsibility to do something about. What a great disease to acquire! Think about cancer as an example. Most people don't have control over whether their cancer gets better. There are things that can be done and choices that can be made, but I think it's reasonably well understood that cancer is not a disease that living a different way of life will necessarily cure. I'm sure there's a deeper discussion to be had on this subject, but we'll leave it here for now.

Let's look at addiction. I, as well as countless others, have overcome addictions. Many haven't, to be fair. Does that make it a disease? Does that make it something we have no power over? I don't believe so. Why? Because, although it is difficult to overcome addictions, many have chosen to do so. I use the word "chosen" because it's true. I don't know anyone that has chosen to overcome cancer. I do know and have known hundreds of people who have done some version of the things we're discussing in this book (as well as my first book, *When I Stop Fighting*) and have overcome addiction. I'm not aware of a book or a way of living that will cure cancer. I do believe there are ways to more likely keep from getting cancer, but not a handbook to cure it. Again, probably a topic for another time.

There are other reasons why I don't believe we are dealing with a disease when we're discussing addiction. Most don't start their addicted lives as fully blown addicts out of the gate. There is a progression that takes place, and it goes something like this: For me, although my first drink felt great, initially I was dealing with a preference; then it became a compulsion; then, after indulging enough, an addiction. There was a clear progression. I chose it, I exacerbated it, and I kept doing it, to my own detriment. The fact that many of us have done it so often and with such fervor is, in my opinion, not the fault of some disease, it's on us. It's also on us to rectify it.

The overwhelming reason I have an issue with calling addiction a "disease" is because it harkens back to a destructive practice we've already discussed: blame. By throwing blame into the arena of our life, we absolve ourselves from wielding one of our most valuable assets: our responsibility. If we use blame as the wedge between us and our responsibility, we give away all our power to change and improve ourselves.

Some of us will hide behind blame and defend ourselves, and our addiction(s), till the day we die. The sad news is, many will die of their addiction or because of their addiction.

It's not a secret that drug and alcohol abuse is of epidemic proportions. It's no secret that we have an obesity epidemic here in the US that continues to escalate.

Some of us will wake up to the fact that we have everything we need to overcome addiction and embrace the power that's already built into us. The only questions to ask are, "Who are we going to be?" and "What are we willing to do to get there?"

Final thoughts on disease and addiction. Whether or not we subscribe to addiction as a disease or not, there are facts that remain true: The doctor isn't going to fix addiction; there's no drug to cure addiction; the only way to overcome it is through a change in our mind, heart, and soul. Anything we try to do to sidestep that truth is, in my opinion, a failure to scrutinize and be forthright with ourselves.

As we've seen, being honest with ourselves is paramount to a successful, intentional, conscious way of living, as well as the catalyst for affecting real, lifetime change. We're free to choose any direction or trajectory we prefer. Along the way we'll be revising our beliefs, and many things that we thought we knew will be set aside. They'll likely be replaced with convictions and principles that make sense and provide structure and function in our everyday lives. We'll allow ourselves to ask questions and search for answers that make sense for us as individuals, not just what makes sense to the crowd. It's always worth looking, it's always worth questioning what we believe. Maybe our thoughts about politics will no longer determine what we believe. Maybe we stop watching the news. Maybe our relationships with family and friends go through fluctuations. Maybe we focus on building ourselves intentionally and purposefully, and stop accepting as truth what we've learned up to this point or what we see on TV or on our phones. Or even what we may have learned from family and friends.

When we do that for a time (I recommend long enough to become strong in our revised beliefs and outlook), we can come back to some of the old systems with a fresh outlook. We can peer behind the curtain again at some of the things we used to believe and see them for what they are. Instead of being molded by news or politics or social media, and those things becoming our belief system, we create our own belief system and determine what fits for us. Or we can jettison them altogether and continue our journey. At that point, we will not be stuck anymore, we'll have choices. There's no better place to be inside of ourselves than having choices as to what we believe and internalize. This is otherwise known as freedom.

CHAPTER FIVE

A LITTLE LANTERN

W e've examined the concept of humility and how this is indispensable to our journey. The interesting thing is, we will keep receiving lessons about being humble and accepting direction, especially as long as we refuse to listen. It's fascinating how life attempts to aim us in the direction that is ultimately best for us. The only question is, do we listen? Remember the example of our trajectory as it relates to using our GPS? That little voice will try to get us to go in a particular direction, even correct us when we're off track.

After a distraction or an unexpected incident, it's easy to get frustrated, stay off track. Many times, we could just listen but decide not to. If we don't, we keep getting the lessons as life continues to rattle our cage. I happen to be one who has needed my cage rattled and shaken and sometimes tipped over before I'd pay attention and truly listen. What does "listening" mean? It means revising the way we do things based on the lessons being shown to us. Until we really work to integrate this foundational concept into the fabric of how we move through our days, we will continue to struggle and flail when it comes to affecting change.

We briefly touched on the fact that we'll need to gather some tools as we embark upon this journey. There are a great number of things that we'll need to pay attention to as we go. In getting started, though, there are some basics that will make sense not only to be aware of, or perhaps become reacquainted with, but begin to think about, ponder, and integrate into our every day.

These are not hard and fast rules per se, but if we've never made a conscious decision and effort to align with them, then as we do and as we get better at it, we'll find that we are in a completely different ballgame than what we'd become accustomed to.

To find ourselves in a place where we're willing to learn, consciously grow, and intentionally do things differently, we'll need an oft misunderstood ally with us every step of the way, but particularly when we begin. It's easy to be run down by fears, by old ways of thinking, and by habits we're attempting to break, but if we have this ally with us, the journey becomes much more palatable.

Humility

I have heard for a long time that humility is another word for "teachable"; however, people often misunderstand humility and equate it with weakness or submissiveness. Could this be true? I suppose it could, but not for our purposes and how we will be garnering and utilizing humility as a powerful weapon in our cache.

What happens when we're teachable? What happens when we finally admit that we don't have all the answers or, for that matter, any of the answers? That's the starting point if we're ready to change. If it's not, then we're not sick and tired of being sick and tired … yet.

Letting go of preconceived notions or things we think we know is paramount to our success in the realm of living a contented, abundant life. How else do we learn? How else do we decide we need to change and, more than that, decide we are going to change? This brand of change is not available to those who have all the answers. Why would it be? If we think we know it all before we get started, then no change is necessary or possible. Who can be taught that already knows?

Who is willing to do things differently that already has the answers for everyone else and assumedly themselves?

We can't give anyone humility. We can't make anyone teachable. We can, though, present the tools and plant the seeds so that when someone is willing to change, and ready to change, they know they need to put a cork in it and utilize humility. I say "utilize" and not "become" because we need, first, to know humility exists as an option and as a tool; and, second, make the choice to listen and learn as opposed to "know." Then comes number three somewhere down the line, which, if we're consciously practicing the first two for a while, the natural next step is "become."

Please understand when I use the word "become," I am not referring to a time and a place where humility or any other principle happens, like a score in basketball or football. It's always a process and it's always "becoming," which is great news. "Becoming" means there's no end to the depth of what we can experience. There's no place we can't go and there's nothing we can't manifest inside ourselves. This is welcome news as we won't reach the end of the pool or the bottom of the ocean. We can work on and with these tools forever and keep experiencing, growing, and sharing till the proverbial cows come home.

That's where the principle of humility turns into the opposite of what we would normally equate with the concept, that of submissiveness or weakness. There are weak people out there, and there are submissive people out there. I wouldn't call those people necessarily humble. When we're truly humble in our life, we become powerful. We become open, eager, and willing to listen. We're not hung up on what we assume we know. We're not trying to prove something in our conversations. We're not chomping at the bit to be right or impress others with what we think. The entire universe of knowledge and wisdom opens because we don't know.

It is powerful to be the "dumbest person in the room." Now I don't mean that literally, but what a weight off our shoulders if we don't need to dominate conversations and we don't need to be looking around like a one-eyed dog at a barbeque trying to find people to impress. There's no anxiety when we're comfortably conscious of and absorbing our surroundings, the people, the universe. It's a way of being in the moment because we're observing in moments, not having our brain feverishly trying to figure out what we want to say next and to whom.

(I'll be going deeper into these paradoxes that we rarely appreciate or give life to in my third book, *The Fighting Stops*.)

Suffice it to say that humility gets our front end aligned. It puts us on the road in a reliable first vehicle and allows us to join the game of life in a different mode. When we become aware that this indispensable tool exists and begin to pay attention and utilize it, there's no limit to where teachable can take us. A mighty tool in our evolving arsenal that will be with us forever as we consciously alter our trajectory.

Courage

To me, courage sounds like an outdated word. I mean, who needs courage these days? It's not like we need to go out and take down a mastodon or prepare to be attacked by a neighboring tribe. None but a very few of us, who are courageous in that way, need to worry about that brand of courage. Most of us will never need to call up that kind of intestinal fortitude or face the circumstances that would require it.

Have we become lazy because we don't need to call up our courage often or ever? Have we gotten so used to things being handed to us that we don't even try to do anything difficult? It's not like we must hunt for food, water, or shelter to stay alive, right?

What about the courage to admit and accept that what we've been doing isn't working? What about the courage, once we've admitted those things, to embark upon the seemingly impossible task of changing how we do things? Changing how we think about things? Risking the loss of friends and possibly family members (but maybe gaining new friends in the process!)? These things unequivocally require courage, especially at the beginning.

There's this whole field of things before us that's uncommon, unexplored, unusual territory, and when we begin to feel things that are atypical and terrifying based on what we've been used to, it, in a word, sucks.

In the case of addictions, perhaps we're feeling things for the first time. We may have numbed feelings for so long that once we start to feel again, it's all new. I can attest to the disturbing nature of allowing myself to feel again. To drop the things from my life that kept me from feeling too much and then being slapped in the face with uncertainty, doubt, worry, and anger all hanging off my sleeve, at the age of 19. To continue to move forward and not give up in the face of these things requires courage. "This too shall pass" comes to mind again, as a remedy for those times when we'd rather set aside whatever courage we've mustered and run back to what got us into trouble in the first place.

It's very important to note that everything passes through good times and tough times. In the tough times we can rest assured that if our courage wanes, solace can be found in knowing that whatever is kicking our emotions around the room will pass. Solace can also be found in knowing that as we move forward in a different way of doing and responding, life gets significantly more manageable and more peaceful, despite what's happening around us.

The courage to "stay the course" and keep going to the best of our ability is what separates those who get some or all of the "wishlist" from those who don't. In an age of instant gratification and high expectations of everything outside us, it takes courage to trust in a process, to trust that it takes time to realize change. It takes courage to set aside the expectations, look to those with experience and wisdom, and trust that we will get to a better place by doing the work and using the tools utilized by those who achieved before us. Courage is one of those tools.

It is easy sometimes to assume that tools like courage lie outside of us somehow and are unreachable. Not true. Courage is something we can call up within ourselves and is very accessible if we are willing to utilize it. I'm reminded of a time when I've heard people beg and plead for God to give them the strength or courage to do a thing. I believe that God has already bestowed within us the courage and strength; we just stopped believing it or never truly understood it in the first place. We can call upon the courage and strength that lie within us anytime we want.

I am reminded of Gandalf in *The Lord of the Rings*, facing the demon in the cave, when he lifts his staff above his head with both arms and slams it into the stone. "*You shall not pass!*" Why can't we do that? What about the demons we must face? We can do that, but it takes a decision to be courageous. It takes a decision to not be tossed around by the never-ending influences, pulling and pushing us this way and that. We are taught that everything is outside us and that life happens and there's not much we can do other than react with whatever emotion or response seems appropriate at any given moment.

To an extent this is true, at least the part where "life happens," but what if we train ourselves to act as opposed to react; to respond based on the strength inside us as opposed to the constantly changing forces outside us? It's possible and there are many around us who live in just that way. I am often reminded that I don't need to ask God for strength or courage. I've already been given strength and courage. This is where, if we truly have faith, we use it. It's not up to God; it's up to us to call up what we're already given.

Perseverance

What happens when we don't see or feel the changes we're expecting right away? Do we go back to the old way of doing things? Do we shrug our shoulders, sigh, and give up, thinking we gave it a good try? No. The only people who fail in this journey are the ones who quit. The ones who give up. What kept me going sometimes was remembering what one of my mentors said, "Don't give up before the miracle." I kept believing that there was something just around the next corner that felt better, that was better than being lost and miserable. Even if it was just feeling a little better, that for me was a miracle at that time. I knew the road that lay behind me and didn't want to go back to that. I was excited about the road that lay in front of me although it was nebulous, unfamiliar, and scary. They told me this way of life would be much better, and I believed them. They told me it would take time, and I believed them, mostly. I certainly had my doubts, especially when things got tough, and life threw a few curve balls. There was no longer a place to suppress or muffle the emotions I'd rather not feel. I couldn't just run and hide like I used to. I had to face life on life's terms and work on me. That was the commitment, and my intention was to do just that.

This is where perseverance comes in. It can be "easy" to quit what doesn't feel good. That might work, at least for a while. Running and hiding has some appeal. Conversely, just because we don't like it or don't *want* to face it doesn't mean it's not good for us. If we're being confronted with difficulty, which is a normal occurrence, it's because we need to confront it and work through it. There's something we need to learn so that we can move forward to the next level. It is our opportunity to improve and strengthen something about ourselves and our ability to not only withstand but perhaps even thrive through the next hurdle. If we run and hide, we can rest assured that we will stay on the merry-go-round of not getting too far in our emotional growth or mental toughness, both necessary attributes of a sturdy, mature human being.

Our trajectory toward True North requires perseverance. Lying down and giving up just prolongs the possibility of correction toward our ultimate objective and as we've discussed, the longer we're on an unintentional, aimless track, the further we veer from True North. Building intestinal fortitude through perseverance and intention in our purpose will serve to strengthen us anytime things get tough moving forward, and I promise you, they will get tough. We're deliberately building our tool chest to withstand whatever life throws at us. Sometimes we won't believe we can get through a rough spot. That's okay. Toughing it out is just a part of the process sometimes, until we get to a point where we begin to believe, and our experience changes because we persevered.

Crossroads and Clarity

When I'm cluttered up with all the things I think matter, or that I think will get me what I'm looking for in this life, based on what I've been taught and conditioned to believe, it's difficult to gain the clarity necessary to ask myself the important questions. Then, to honestly answer those questions, for myself.

There's an unconscious nature to many things that cause us to suffer, including living our life on a daily basis. We're conditioned to never observe, peruse, or question what we do and why we do it. Do addicted people want to be addicted? No. They spend much of their time trying to convince the world that they're not. This is the nature of addiction; trying to convince everyone, including the addicted person, that it's not there. We can all be looking right at it, but to preserve itself, it must try to convince everyone it doesn't exist. Many times, it's successful, especially with the addicted person.

We can go along, day by day, month by month, maybe decade by decade, doing what we do and not questioning it. This is the nature of unconscious living, and until there's some consequence, we can be unconscious forever.

To awaken, to become conscious, means we look at our life in an intentional and awakened state. We lead with honesty, not defensiveness. We become open and at least begin to understand that there might be a different or better way forward for us.

Sometimes we come to a crossroads. Sometimes things get very clear, at least for a short spell. We ask ourselves why we're doing what we're doing and have the capacity and clarity in those moments to answer honestly. These are the times when we can effect change for ourselves. These are the moments when that little voice is helping us along, asking us to pay attention. Asking us to take a sincere peek and possibly make a change. What might this look like?

"Why do I feel so lonely?" "Do I smoke too much weed?" "I'm waiting for the courage to start that venture." "I'm drinking a lot lately." "I'm scared to take that risk." "I know eating so much is bad for me, why can't I stop?"

My first experience with crossroads goes back to when I was 18 years old. I'd been slated for a drug and alcohol treatment program and had about a month until I was scheduled to be there. I'd be 19 by the time I went in. I kept up the drinking and drugging, fully intending to go through this treatment experience and get right back to my destructive lifestyle or not go through the treatment program, which would damage and possibly sever ties with my parents. The messed-up thing was, I didn't recognize it as destructive at that time. It was just what I'd become used to and what all of my friends did. I'm sure those in the throes or those who've overcome addiction can relate.

As the days drew closer, I'd be sitting around with my friends, discussing, over whatever substances we imbued ourselves with, next steps. It's an interesting round table discussion to envision.

"Well, you can just do what I did and go through it, then get back to partying with us."

"Move in with me and don't even go through that bullshit."

"That treatment shit doesn't even work anyway."

The wisdom flowed from their well-meaning but clueless beings. They didn't know any better and neither did I. We'd just graduated from high school less than a year ago. Our heads were very far up our asses ...

Something changed for me in those last few days. I was able to feel the misery underlying my devil-may-care demeanor. I was able to catch a glimpse, however fleeting, of the pain I'd caused and the people who worried about me. I had a brief moment of clarity, and a speck of light shone through the door. Enough to help me begin to want to uncover whether there was anything different for me out there.

Standing at a crossroads, unaware that in the midst of the darkness enveloping me, I was holding a little lantern. The lantern was barely giving enough light to see, but that trace of light was a beginning for me. That trace of light was, however miniscule, a bit of clarity. A moment where I could consider something different. Consider that I might need help.

What was on the other side? What was down those roads? No idea.

I decided to go to drug and alcohol treatment, a formidable and daunting prospect.

These can be grueling and challenging times, difficult moments. They can also be the moments where we decide we're sick and tired of being sick and tired. They can be the moments when, if we embrace and truly accept that we may need some changes, the most momentous transformations can start to happen in our life. One little spark, one little moment of clarity and honesty can transform that trajectory, if we begin at that moment to start a more difficult, but infinitely more rewarding path.

The good news and I suppose the bad news is, we are gifted these moments of clarity so that we can change our trajectory. We are presented with these crossroads so that we have an opportunity to revise our behaviors and our perceptions, setting us up for adjustments to how we choose to live our life. Why else would we have them? Why else would there ever be a question within us as to what we're doing and why we're doing it?

If we're willing to take an honest look, we must ask ourselves why trajectories in our life even exist? Why do some of us start on social media at the age of 14 and become completely consumed with it by the age of 16, spending ten hours per day on our phones? How is it we could have just a few beers at age 16 and be dealing coke by age 19? Why are some of us a few pounds overweight at 32, and by forty we're a hundred pounds overweight? Conversely, there are plenty of examples of a person embracing a principled life at 26 and becoming a successful business owner at thirty. Or those who might feel themselves heading down an addictive path, so they consciously rein it in. How can this be? Is the direction of my life, complete with all that I contribute and all that I fail to contribute, a thing? Can I choose which direction I want to go?

Absolutely is the answer to both of those questions. In those moments of clarity, those crossroads, what am I choosing?

CHAPTER SIX

THE WRONG TREE

S o, we've come to the juncture where we feel like there may be aspects of our life that could benefit from some adjustments. How do we start? How do we effect that change we need in our life?

Let's begin by getting crystal clear on one thing, perhaps the most difficult pill to swallow: We will not incur one ounce of change in our own life by focusing attention on what we surmise *other* people need to do. That simply won't work. It's time to pull our horns in and place the focus inward. Nothing will change in our life by placing blame or adopting the attitude of a victim. We give away every ounce of power we possess to transform *ourselves* when we try to place the onus on others or on circumstances. The very nature of placing blame or adopting a victim mentality is the opposite of taking responsibility for ourselves and what we need to do to improve and convert *our* world. If we're clear on those simple truths, it will help to illuminate the path to moving forward in a constructive, meaningful way.

It takes strength and it takes the courage we discussed previously to begin the journey of change. Make no mistake, we must start. We may not feel we have the strength or the courage to begin to change or do things differently, but I promise you that we all do. It is not a matter of whether we possess the strength to do a thing; it is a matter of whether we summon and utilize the strength that already lies within us to begin to approach our life in a different manner. People do change and they do modify their trajectory. It usually begins at the point of being willing to admit we need to change and that we need help. We have to keep in mind those moments of clarity, we have to keep in mind why we came to the crossroads and how that felt. It can be easy to slip back into the unconscious behavior that got us here. It can be easy to set aside the feeling we had when we desired change. If we allow ourselves to succumb to our unwillingness this time, then we'll probably have to wait for another crossroads, another moment of clarity.

It is important to understand that each time we ignore or fail to act upon life "rattling our cage," the trajectory we're currently on will not change and will probably steepen in its bearing away from True North. Do I want to begin to change what I know I need to change now, knowing that if I wait, things will likely get worse? That's the question, and that's where utilizing our inherent strength begins even though we may not realize we possess that strength.

I have a simple example of the strength I already possess but, in this instance, failed to use:

I do not like the dentist. I've had an issue with my gums not getting numb enough before the drilling starts, so for thirty-plus years, I've felt the drilling while having a cavity addressed. This never sat well with me.

I'd tell the story to each dentist, "Just so you know, I don't get totally numb, and I feel the drilling. What are the options?"

"Well, there's no reason why you shouldn't get numb. Let's try it. I'll go slow with the drill, and you raise your hand if you feel anything," was the typical speech accompanying another attempt with only one shot.

Inevitably, I'd feel it, and sometimes I'd change dentists, other times I wouldn't.

A couple of times I'd get a dentist who did what I needed, but then I'd inevitably re-locate and have to do the whole thing again.

A few years ago, I cracked a tooth and had to have it filled. It was a huge filling and the dentist explained to me that at some point when the filling cracks or fails, which it's sure to do, I'd need to have that tooth extracted and an alternate tooth installed. The dentist thought it would probably be within a year. Well, the filling cracked within a year, and I went back to the same dentist. He said the best thing to do would be to begin the process of extraction and installation of a new tooth. I wimped out and asked him to repair that big filling. He obliged but told me that I risked infection and further potential problems if I put off the more difficult path.

It's been four years now, and I cracked that filling again, several months ago. I knew that I needed to get back to the dentist and handle this the proper way. The clarity slapped me in the face several times, and I pushed it aside, procrastinating. Even as I tasted the infection coming from that tooth, I held off, not wanting to go through the temporary pain of addressing it the proper and responsible way. I knew that by addressing it, the final product would be a clean bill of health for that tooth and subsequently, for the trajectory of my mouth and dental health. Well, several years later, I still hadn't addressed it. Finally, as I was writing this book, I scolded myself for being such a wimp and promptly called the dentist to set up the appointment. Getting the tooth out and addressing the issue I'd purposefully ignored, was a wrestling match for about three hours in the dentist chair, as the unseen damage and decay of the tooth became evident. There was an abscess under the tooth and the problem is still not resolved. More trips to the dentist in my near future.

Do I feel sorry for myself? No. Do I blame anyone or feel like a victim? No. This is 100% on me, I was just being a coward. The strength to suck it up and pick up the phone years ago to address that situation properly was something I possessed, I just failed to do it, and now I pay whatever price there is to pay. It wasn't that I lacked the strength, it was that I didn't utilize the strength I already had. The silver lining is I learned that if I have three shots to numb my mouth, I don't feel a thing. Now, I insist on three shots.

This is a very simple example of not utilizing or ignoring the strength I have, and there have been other examples over 38 years of sobriety from alcohol and drugs. Many times, I've had to suck it up and experience the pain when I didn't want to. Many times, I've been paralyzed by fear of not wanting to do something and had to do it anyway to stay sober. The dentist hesitancy is an anomaly for me but is a great reminder that I must always pay attention and be willing to go through things, as opposed to backing away from them or detouring around them, just because they may not feel good. Like the previously decaying tooth in question, it isn't going away on its own. The importance of vigilance, paying attention, and consciously living cannot be over-emphasized.

I used to do business with a guy in the early 2000s who used to say to prospective clients, "Above all, if we end up working together and there's ever a problem, let us know right away. We don't want any issues to fester."

Two valuable takeaways for me in those words: (1) You never know from whence bits of valuable wisdom might come, so pay attention; and (2) unaddressed items in life always fester, so handle them.

I have been reminded time after time as I've traversed this mortal coil that the strength is already in me. It's up to me to believe it and then utilize it. When I move forward, start, forge ahead, whatever you want to call it, I can then look back, smile, and understand that every time I utilize what's in me, I get even stronger for the next time.

So, what does "start" mean? Okay, I need the strength to start, but start what? Here's the simple answer, which we will expand upon as this book continues: Start to do things differently; start to ask for help; start to admit you don't have all the answers. There's a myriad of answers or at least help and direction, available for the asking. If I have an issue with alcohol or drugs, there are support groups available. If I have an issue with food, same thing, plenty of help and resources are available. If I struggle with anxiety or fears or gambling or addictions of any sort, all I have to do is reach out, especially in the age of having every answer at our fingertips. It may be as simple as starting that project or making that phone call or doing something I've been procrastinating for years. I understand that it's one thing to discuss and much more difficult to do. Simple does not mean easy, I get it. Again, we must ask ourselves what staying on the same course will yield. Highly likely it will yield nothing better than it did before, and more probable is that life will continue to get worse.

I got sober in a time of payphones and having to go to a library to research topics and subjects. There were plenty of resources available to me at that time to get and stay sober, and today, I assume we can multiply the availability and convenience of resources by at least a factor of ten. So, what's the reason why so many people continue to struggle and fail to replace their trajectory with a different direction?

Because we live in a society where ease, convenience, and the absence of any pain whatsoever is always the goal. We never see an invention that touts the fact that it's going to make our life more difficult or even challenging. It's always what's going to make life easier. Been happening forever and that's absolutely contributing to why we have more mental illness, anxiety, obesity, and addictions of every sort. We need challenge, we need difficulty, so that we can face these things and triumph.

We also have a society that seems to value, appease, and sometimes applaud mediocrity. It seems the timeless reverence and value of the distinction between graceful and refined women and masculine and strong men may have come to end. At least for the foreseeable future. It's just easier to be mediocre; it's easier to eat whatever we want, especially if it's convenient and tastes good. It's easier to spark up a joint than face difficult emotions. It's easier to take a pill to make us feel good for a while than it is to go through the arduous process of self-discovery and healing. It's easier to let our parents do the tough job of paying the bills and keeping up the house than it is getting off our butt and moving out and doing it for ourselves. It's easier and more socially acceptable these days to justify and celebrate mediocrity than it is to embrace strength.

There also appears to be more adults embracing and perpetuating behaviors that were once thought to be the folly of youth. The hiding behind drugs—illicit, legal, or prescription—by people in their forties, fifties, and beyond, is alarming. The futility of hiding from life via these fallacious means is difficult to watch, especially when they are friends or family members. These people will stay stuck in emotional and spiritual kindergarten and be applauded for it. Not us. Not those with whom we can experience and share this journey.

To change and move toward a life of deep meaning, strong relationships, and inner peace and contentment, we must commit to doing difficult things. We must commit to going through the pain of discovering a new way, a way which we are likely not familiar with and don't feel we're ready for. We must commit to throwing away the crutch and, over time, maybe additional crutches. It's the only way.

If we think we're going to embark upon a more successful, happy, contented way of life by doing the same things that got us the life we're trying to change, it's highly likely we're barking up the wrong tree. Is this bad news? No! On the contrary, it's great news! It's great news because there is another way. I'm not shackled by my current life or lifestyle if I choose not to be. I'm not bound to my current trajectory if I decide not to be and then do the work to prove that out.

Everything we want to do or try to do that doesn't align with how we were raised or with what we currently believe is a risk. It is very easy to continue in the groove that was cut for us, or to which we've become accustomed, and just do that forever.

"I'm just not feeling in any way fulfilled or challenged being a broker anymore," I said to Kristina, my wife, somewhere around 2010.

"Well, what are you going to do?"

"I honestly don't know. We've got mortgages, the money is good, how the heck am I going to replace that income, not to mention, take care of all these financial responsibilities?"

"We'll figure it out," was the supportive reply.

"Made it this far, I suppose."

I'd taken a lot of risks to go from being a very blue-collar kid, raised in Michigan, starting at zero, to being a successful businessperson, living outside Boston. The decisions to get out of my comfort zone and stay out of my comfort zone were numerous. Not to mention, I needed to stay sober and continue to grow, upgrade, and improve myself, to the best of my ability. Sobriety requires this if we're going to have any semblance of serenity and peace in our life.

Kristina and I decided, perhaps against better judgement, especially as concerns financial matters, that we were going to leave our current occupations. We were both paid very well, not to mention we had a large amount of monthly bills we needed to ensure we kept up with. What exactly was on the other side of taking the risk to leave? We did not know.

Sometimes the call is louder than the fears and sometimes we listen to the call. This was one of those times. When the pain of staying put is greater than the projected pain (at least we hope) of doing things differently, there really is no choice. Staying can mean a serious blow to our trajectory, because it feels like, and in many cases is, giving up. Leaving can potentially mean difficulty with uncertainty, finances, learning something new, etc. The big difference is, planting our foot in the ground and moving into a new adventure can be exhilarating and adventurous, and we can achieve a sense of satisfaction, no matter the difficulty. Staying put will very likely not yield such trajectory enhancement.

So, we ended up leaving what we'd become used to for about twenty years each, in order to buy a flailing restaurant and an abandoned investment property. Both of these ventures, which became *ad*ventures, needed major rehabilitation. We knew nothing of the restaurant business and had no idea how the real estate venture would work out.

Isn't that the point of risk-taking though? We're not supposed to know how everything is going to work out, nor can we. We just need to know that we're going to do our part to ensure they do.

Fast forward almost a dozen years. The risks we embarked upon did work out, for which we are grateful.

It can be difficult to start and then it can be difficult to continue to take the risks presented to us. Why? Because once we've gone a ways down the road of risk and the subsequent change, there's a comfort zone that can develop.

"Really, I have to keep doing this shit?" I think to myself jokingly from time to time when presented with a challenge or another difficult life-changing direction or idea. "Yes, you do. You love it," I retort. And it's true, I really do. I've worn myself out and worn myself down many times since embarking on the journey of change. Sometimes I just need to rest for a bit, which I've learned to do, but I wouldn't trade this adventure for anything.

Let's get back to your adventure.

Is it easy, convenient, or fun? No, especially in the beginning. Is it one of the most, if not *the* most fulfilling and fruitful journeys you can take part in? It is, without a doubt. It puts you in a rare position as an inhabitant of this planet because very few of the people you currently know or will ever meet assume this journey. Why? Because at first, it's not easy, it will not fit with anything else you've ever tried, and it can be tough, at least for a while. At first it might feel like wriggling out of an ill-fitting and uncomfortable skin. It will likely involve the pain of taking an honest and open appraisal of what got you where you are and why. It will be the opposite of what most of your friends and family do. On this point I want to be very clear: This is not a judgment of friends or family, it is not saying that what you do or what they do is any better or worse than the other. It's simply different. It's merely moving toward a conscious way of living, a decision to look behind the curtain of what got you to the point where you might start to want to change. It is the decision for yourself and whatever time you have left here to determine if there is anything else other than what you've been doing and what you would keep doing had you not been introduced to something different.

This is where a little blind faith might come in handy, before we start to develop actual faith, which we will speak about soon. Sometimes a little "fake it till you make it" can apply here. For now, to get started, it's a matter of acknowledging that what we've been doing is not working; we need some help; we're willing to try like hell to live without the crutches, and embrace a different, conscious, and, for the moment, more difficult path.

What's the reward? Well, I guess we can go back to the "wishlist." Is it worth a little rough going to come out on the other side and, over time, achieve things you hadn't even dreamed of? I assure you that it is. To get to a point where you can confidently say that you have no regrets; appreciate life, even the struggles; and look forward to what's next. Here are a few of the things you can reap from developing yourself and your life in an intentional way:

- Waking up every day with a smile on your face, looking forward to the day

- Feeling like whatever happens next is going to be interesting and if not, at the very least, instructional

- Having that "hole" in the middle of your chest filled with gratitude

- Having your body, mind, heart, and soul attended to and supported by your new way of life

- Feeling comforted and supported in your relationships as well as being comforting and supporting in return

- Feeling like you're strong and ready to accept challenges and take risks

- Accomplishing things you intended to accomplish

- Working toward and accomplishing goals within yourself and how you relate to the rest of the world

- Becoming convinced that this life can be an incredible, fun, rewarding adventure

There are too many others to count, and they will be a little different for everyone, but you get the essence. Life becomes very different when we treat it differently. Wouldn't that be something? Are these things our experience currently? If it's not at least partially how our life is going, perhaps we're ready to try something new, something fulfilling, something with a promise that includes these things. It's a rewarding path, not just filled with momentary distraction or relief, trying to plug the holes in our heart and life. It's a journey that can be filled with contentment and awe as the predominant thread that runs through every aspect of our existence and continues to improve as we consistently pay attention and practice behaviors and principles that support it. Another promise that a new way of life makes is, if we ever want to go back to the old one that we decided to abandon in the first place, it will be there awaiting us, no questions asked. Which direction do we want to go? Are we ready for change?

CHAPTER SEVEN

HERE, BITE DOWN ON THIS STICK

However we've decided to begin traversing this path, whether it's a physical meeting of like-minded people, an online support group, other like-minded gathering or form of support, or just a decision to change what we do and how we do it, setting aside those fears and utilizing our courage, it is crucial that we keep our commitment to that decision. The moment of clarity or that crossroads where we hear that voice inside directing us to our greater good, or at least guiding us away from our potential further destruction, can be fleeting. It's easy to fall into our old behaviors again, painful as they may be. We never know when our cage might be rattled again and when we might be willing to gift ourselves the honesty to be willing enough to consider change. It could be a month, a year, five years, forty years, or never. That's just the truth.

We could go to our grave having never listened or at least never heeded that call to change. Some do go to their graves and it's very unfortunate and very sad because many leave earlier than they should and never gave themselves a chance to truly live. If we don't think that drinking, drugs, the potential for attendant mental illness, food addictions, obesity, gambling, or other obsessions contribute to the destruction of human beings on this planet, we're fooling ourselves. Not just destroyed lives, careers, and families; also destroyed minds, hearts, spirits, and the children they raise to embrace the same behaviors.

It's not about just addictions or obsessions. What about fears, what about the willingness to take risks? Calling upon our strength and courage to start that new business, make that difficult phone call, strike out on our own, or, in my case, go to the dentist? We all could be living our "wishlist," but we must start. We must pay attention, be honest and willing, and start with a fervent commitment.

One of my great mentors said to me long ago, "It's a lonely journey, when you truly embrace a life that very few are willing to embrace. You're not going to find many you'll be able to relate to or that want the same things you do."

I thought, "What do you mean? I have plenty of friends, family, people around who care about me."

As I've continued down this road, I can confirm that he was right on the money. I give the same advice now when I meet a younger person who's embarking on a similar path. I can see how sometimes they'd like to quit, go back to a former way of life.

It's not necessarily a "lonely" journey the way we would normally think of lonely. It's lonely because so few people can relate to putting effort into something more than their appearance and financial condition. I mean, a lot of people read books, but who really cares about clearing the wreckage from their heart or uncovering the dust from their soul? Not too many. That's why it's lonely sometimes. Most are looking for more noise, not less. Especially in the younger years. Who wants to be calm, quiet, and grateful? Again, not too many.

What are some of the tools we'll need to stay on this path once we've made the commitment to begin? Remember, we must internalize and seek to understand that continuing with the same behaviors, attitudes, and adherence to things that got us here will keep us here; they'll keep us stuck. We must remain open to the belief that there's a different way. This is where faith comes in.

Faith

Faith is not necessarily something that has to involve God. I grew up in a very religious household, and what I believe and the faith I maintain has morphed and changed many times, as I've traversed this journey. My faith started as no faith. It began as a commitment to myself to do better and to be better. I relied on people smarter and more experienced than me to show me the way. I had faith in them because they were exhibiting the things in their lives that I wanted in my life. Things I was not previously familiar with such as peace, wisdom, unselfishness, thoughtfulness, and, in some cases, financial security. I wanted these things, so I listened in a spirit of faith, sprinkled with some humility (teachableness) because I finally admitted to myself that I didn't have a clue and I couldn't do it alone. These people were not hampered by petty annoyances or complaints. They did not waste their time blaming or encumbering themselves with a victim mentality. I wanted to be them or at least be able to manifest in my life what they had in their lives. Now not everyone is able to manifest all these attributes, and there should never be an expectation that anyone is perfect or to be placed on a pedestal. I was told early on in my attempt to adopt a different way of living, "Take what you can use and leave the rest." My ability to understand that little gem has transformed over the years as well, as there are different levels of understanding everything, as we know. We are confronted with little gems of wisdom or guidance very often as we enjoy the path of life and do our best to remain open to the wonderful reality that everyone can teach us something. The slightest and seemingly most inconsequential interactions can be interesting seeds of wisdom or, at the very least, get us to think.

"It's very important to keep an open mind and listen to what everyone has to say," a mentor told me early on in my new life.

I was only interested in listening to those I knew were living the life I wanted to live and was not yet familiar with the concept that messages can come from anywhere and anyone.

"Okay," I said, no doubt looking puzzled.

"Someone you might not think can help you, can. You just never know."

Not long thereafter, as I paid better attention to everyone and everything, to the best of my ability, I was amazed at the things I heard that helped make the journey just a bit easier or, at least, a little easier to understand.

"You can't change other people, no matter how bad you think they need it," Tom, a homeless guy, casually imparted to our 12-Step table at the Alano Club one night.

Exactly what I needed to hear as I was currently embroiled in trying to help my sister overcome addiction and some of the related issues.

"All we can change is ourselves," he continued.

Incredible. Those words helped me. They gave me a little bit of breathing room to implement faith. I was beginning to realize that my ideas about what other people needed to do with their lives were meaningless unless they were ready to be helped. If I was beginning to embrace faith for me and my life, I also needed to welcome faith regarding how the rest of the universe was working.

(I heard not too long thereafter, as I asked someone about Tom's welfare, that he was killed in an altercation in a nearby city. RIP, Tom.)

This is another level of faith or perhaps, a manifestation of faith. It's not a coincidence when we begin to look for seeds of wisdom, continued understanding, beauty, and goodness, and find them in our everyday interactions.

Faith can bring us peace of mind, knowing that if we start on a path and have decided to consciously change our trajectory, we're going somewhere other than where we've already been. As we've touched on before, we know what lies behind us, and even though we don't know what lies in front of us, it's okay, especially if we can dip even our little toe in the vat of faith. If we can start with that modicum of confidence, to get us going and get through a couple of hurdles, that reliance on something outside ourselves, also known as faith, grows. We begin to understand that just because something is difficult or scares us, it's very likely not the end of the world. As we move along the path to a new us and a new way of approaching our life, our conviction grows, our confidence grows.

This is an ever-evolving and developing process, and if my experience is used as a guide, it never culminates. Our faith can and will continue to grow as we move consciously forward and place reliance on things unseen. At some juncture, we won't have to know what's ahead, we won't have to try to control the uncontrollable. Where our previous days may have begun in a spirit of fear, uncertainty, and trepidation, they now begin with an inexplicable ease. We go about our life knowing in our gut that all is okay, no matter what. When tough times come, as they always do, they don't define our life. They are just tough times, and we won't need to know anything more than the tough times will pass, as they always do.

If at some point we want to put our reliance on an idea of God from our youth or that we discover as we explore life wide awake, we can. If we put our reliance on something else, that's okay too. Finding something greater than ourselves to begin to rely upon takes a lot of pressure off us, and as we continue that quest, we'll find that it works.

More than likely these systems will morph over time until we settle on whatever works in our daily life.

Patience

Patience is one of those principles that can be learned over time and needs to be practiced. For me it must be consciously called upon, within myself, until I learn that my impatience is just a manifestation of my emotional and spiritual immaturity. When I can get my head around that, it's easier to be patient. There are very few times when the world is going to work the way I want it to in the time frames I dictate.

There are a couple of things that come to mind here, as it pertains to demonstrating patience: (1) Expectations of others are planned disappointments; and (2) if we walk a mile into the woods, we'll need to walk a mile to get out.

One of those has to do with the world outside of me and one has to do with the even larger and more impactful world, inside of me.

Let's think about "expectations" first. Expectations generally have to do with what's outside of us, and they generally have to do with other people. It certainly would be nice if everyone did what we needed them to do in the time frames that are convenient for us. Wouldn't that be great?

There's freedom in being introduced to the notion that there is nothing we can do when it comes to getting other people on board with our expectations of who they are and how they should live their lives. When we stop to think about that, it becomes almost laughable that we suppose we might have any power over others, real or imagined. If we have not been able to do that great of a job with ourselves, then what is it that we believe we can do for them?

The irony is when we do a great job with ourselves, we will understand that we have no control over others. When we can let go of our expectations of others, we find ourselves automatically being patient because we've internalized the truth that we have no dominion whatsoever over others, their lives, their growth, or their time frames. This is where the freedom part comes in. Freedom is getting to the point where we realize that our only real job is ourselves. Our only real job is how we operate in this world. When we operate, knowing that our true mission is to progress and advance ourselves, how we relate to the world and how we treat everyone else is a manifestation of those efforts. As we evolve along those lines, patience follows, peace follows, contentment follows.

It's great to know that our work on ourselves gets us these freedoms, so let's hurry up and get this "working on ourselves" part out of the way! Gotta slow down a little bit here. The greatest rewards we can experience have to do with the work we do with and on ourselves, but it's also difficult work, and it takes time. It takes a lifetime, in fact. That's not meant to be discouraging, but it is meant to be real. If we "walk a mile into the woods, we'll need to walk a mile to get out," is real. Let's just think about that.

It's easy to make a mess of ourselves when we live unconsciously, when we spend our days focused on everything outside us for our happiness or our satisfaction. We may look great on the outside, but the most important measuring stick is, how do we look on the inside? This is where the rubber hits the road and where we garner the courage and the strength, a day at a time, to commit to the journey.

We don't necessarily need to commit to a lifetime, but we need to commit to start. The lifetime part will naturally follow as we begin to change and experience the successes of a fresh way of operating in this world. This is where we can start to consciously cut ourselves some slack and adopt the principle of patience. Starting is tough, and we've probably put ourselves through a lot just to make that decision. Let's stop for a moment and give ourselves credit for that.

As we move forward, things will start to feel better as well as be better … and, truthfully, sometimes they'll feel worse. That's the reality of growth, that's the reality of consciously moving life forward. This is another place where we can cut ourselves some slack and give ourselves the gift of patience. It is important to not be surprised when the tough times or the times that don't feel so good show up. It's going to happen, and it's a natural part of the growing process. Just because we've decided that we're going to change our life doesn't mean that we're not going to experience difficulty and, at times, confusion. Actually, it's the opposite. Living consciously means we're going to experience all of it, and that's great news.

If we are seriously looking for a change, especially if addiction(s) are a manifestation of our malady, our life was or is likely centered around instant gratification. It may have been unconsciously pursued as we just pop that pill, continue to overeat, or smoke that bowl, rarely realizing the truly destructive nature of our actions and the "escape" we've been erroneously relying upon to manage our internal dysfunction. The underlying cauldron of emotional and spiritual upset swirling beneath our inability to free ourselves from these indulgences is what we need to dig into and find a way to heal. Until we do that, we are going to be perennially engaging in destructive behaviors, and, at some point, they'll work against us. They'll transport us down the road to physical, mental, emotional, and spiritual ruin.

Growing our way out of addiction asks for our patience. That mile into the woods can be a tough mile, and that mile out can be equally tough but also promises to be life-altering and enormously rewarding. As we experience the rewards, it becomes easier to keep walking but also easier to be patient with ourselves.

What about our fears? What about stopping ourselves from taking that risk or moving that intention forward? This can be just as damaging and trajectory-affecting as addictions. Not to mention, the longer we submerge ourselves in and wallow in fear, the stronger those demons become. We can retreat into the woods because of our fears and, as we've already learned, if we're not advancing toward True North, we're retreating from it. How long do we want to retreat? How far into the woods are we willing to go?

It's difficult to imagine a life without the paralyzing fears, where we reach out and advance, in lieu of retreat; where we head toward the light as opposed to embracing the shadows. What would it feel like to achieve our first goal, however small it may be? What would it feel like to reach, to embrace what's difficult? I'll tell you: There's no better feeling in the world when we suck it up and consciously move ourselves and our life forward.

Patience with ourselves is very important as we start this journey but to move ourselves from the woods into what will someday prove to be a beautiful, sunny, inviting place, we need to start.

Determination

So, what are the alternatives to our newfound quest to be better than we have been, from wherever we start? We might be embarking from a very bad place in terms of our trajectory and perhaps have been in a downward spiral for a long, long time. Or, maybe we're young and feel we just need some direction and a place to begin. Either way, we must decide that we want to change, and then we need to actually commit to do things differently if we're going to adjust our path. Remember, the further we walk into the woods, the further will be the walk out. I don't mean that literally, of course, but from an emotional and spiritual perspective, to undo the carnage in our life to family, friends, and strangers, as well as the damage to our heart, soul, and in many cases our body and mind, will take commitment, time, and patience. This is where determination comes in. Determination may include clenching our teeth, biting down on a stick, or screaming out in the woods to rid ourselves of some of the pain and difficulty that changing ourselves can render.

The good news is, as we begin and for a while thereafter, which will be different for everyone, we may have to lean on a universal truth we've touched on previously: This too shall pass. The tough times do pass, but the bad news is, so do the easy times, until we start to practice a new way with discipline and consistency and reap the benefits with more reliability. This does happen, I promise, and is good to bear in mind as we traverse what can be a difficult journey. There will be times when we don't believe it and we get mired in our own feelings about how challenging a new way of life can be. This is completely normal, and it doesn't mean we're failing. In fact, it likely means the opposite. It likely just means we're growing, and as we continue to reach new outcroppings on our way to the summit, we may fall back, we may scare the hell out of ourselves, we may want to quit. Not allowed. Quitting is the only way to fail. As long as we maintain the willingness, through determination and through the inner strength we've garnered to this point, we are on a different trajectory, and we are on the path. Sometimes that's difficult to believe, but it's true.

Back to the question at hand: What are the alternatives? Well, we can always have our misery refunded. We can always go back to numbing ourselves with alcohol, drugs, food, sex, attention, whatever distracts us from contact and relationship with ourselves and our life via our heart and soul. Or we can let fear and hesitation stop us from taking risks or doing things differently. Either way, we're stunting the journey. If we're reading this book and have internalized or related to what it purports, then that alternative seems like a dead-end street because we've been there and done it, right? What did that path do for us before? It brought us here. What's it going to do next time we try the same thing? It's going to put us deeper in the woods with a longer journey to get out again. As we discussed previously, it might be a month, a year, twenty years, or never. We don't know if we'll come back.

What about trying a different replacement for the way we feel? What if our escape had been alcohol, but we're going to try weed or shrooms or any number of other substances that can distract us from how we feel? I've seen this a lot, and the only problem with that "solution" is that those replacements are the same damn thing! It really doesn't matter the justification or the reasoning, the problem is our inability to face life without the crutch, which degrades everything eventually. Our body suffers, our mind suffers, our heart suffers, and our spirit suffers. We go deeper in the woods, and the deeper we go, the likelier it is we can be lost for good. I hate to say that, but it's true. I've seen it many, many times. I've also seen many, many times where a person embraces a real solution to their trajectory issue, they make their way out of the woods, heading again in the direction of True North, and truly begin to enjoy this thing we call life.

"Daryl, I just don't know where to turn right now or what to do," my brother explained. His despair and uncertainty were palpable. "I gotta move out from where I'm at and figure out how to make a better living."

This was almost 25 years ago.

"Well, I know you mentioned maybe starting a landscaping gig. Why not that?" I pleaded, reaching for something to try to help move him from the quagmire of emotion and uncertainty.

"I don't know," was his reply. "I'm just so sick and tired of the bullshit, and I can't stand where I live. I just …" He sounded exasperated and without much hope.

I offered what I could but more than anything, I tried to let him vent. I'd never heard him like that. I was very concerned about him. He was stuck and afraid to move. I've been there too, and it's a tough place to be.

"It's darkest before the dawn," is one I've had to call upon when things seemed most bleak, and I believe this is where Kevin was at this point in his life. He was at a crossroads. No better place to change his trajectory.

Since that time, Kevin has owned and flipped several homes, and has a landscaping business that provides him with a good income and a solid living. He is not the nut job I am when it comes to risk-taking, but he is a perfect example of someone who was in a very tough place and worked his way out of it, forever changing his trajectory.

Much about Kevin has changed since, and he is in a great place and on a solid track. He has turned into one of the most kind-hearted people I know. (He was not always that way.)

Everything about us is a gift. We are designed to utilize our mind, body, heart, and soul as aspects of ourselves to be honored and respected, not to be cast aside and ignored or otherwise abused or abandoned. To ply ourselves with substances or food, feel sorry for ourselves, or wonder why life is so difficult or bad is to miss the point of why we're here. We're here to feel good and bad, we're here to move, we're here to be awed by the beauty around us and connect with it. We're not here to be afraid to move forward or hide somewhere, hoping the world and other people miraculously change so that we're happy, fulfilled, and successful. It just doesn't work that way. We're here to do the work, adhere to a code, and improve ourselves. Flailing and stopping ourselves is our choice; not improving is our choice. So is calling up determination and perseverance when we need them.

Trying and failing, or at least not achieving what we're aiming for, is an essential aspect, not to mention function, of the journey. I say "function" here because at first, we may feel like we're defeated and plummeting toward oblivion when all that's truly happening is, we're experiencing the journey itself. We're not going to climb the mountain without sliding back a little, or a lot. We're not going to experience the view from the summit unless we put in the miles, stare at a lot of rocks, hang off the edge sometimes, and maybe even encounter a bear or two. Just because we've decided we want a different life doesn't by any stretch mean we don't have to pay the mandatory price. Sometimes that price is going to be going through a lot of shit that we'd rather not go through.

When I was doing sales and was in the midst of a very competitive, demanding career, there were many times I didn't feel like going through the tough stuff. In the beginning, it's mostly grueling. As you start to get some wins behind you, it gets easier, or at the very least, there's an understanding that the tough stuff isn't going to kill us. In fact, it makes us more durable. The point is, once you start and get a couple small wins, it's a lot easier to hunt down the next win. Then the wins get bigger, which furthers your resolve and determination.

I've said to many people over the years who were searching for success in their lives, "If you want more than what you have now or more than what most people have, prepare yourself for more difficulty and more headaches, at least for a while, as you get started." That's just how it is. That's just the journey.

We can maintain and call up our determination and feel good about it when "this too [does] pass" because it always does. Then the next time we need to get over a hurdle, it will be easier because we did it before. It's an old axiom, but "nobody ever said life was going to be easy," so why do we expect it to be? Why can't we ride out the tough times and come out the other side improved and strengthened, with our trajectory intact? We can, through the principle of determination.

Consistency

Consistency is the next logical step after faith, patience, and determination. If we make the commitment to consistency, it will, in turn, make the commitment to us. If we've espoused determination in our life and have become willing to do whatever it takes to move ourselves and our life forward, consistency is what brings us to another level. If our past has been characterized by consistently engaging in unhealthy pursuits, whether it's being paralyzed by fears, addictions, or our own self-interest, it is easy to see where that has landed us. Being consistent with damaging behaviors is just as powerful in manifesting a poor trajectory as being consistent with good behaviors is in getting our trajectory straightened out. It is amazing, when we are being true to ourselves and executing nourishing behaviors on a reliable basis, how life feels and how our entire world changes.

Momentum is real and it manifests to drive us in the direction we decide to consistently pursue. When we're determining our trajectory and we take that little walk down memory lane, we can see where the momentum has manifested in our life. "Why is my entire paycheck being gambled away every week when I used to just get a couple scratch tickets on my way home from work?" "How did I get hooked on cocaine when all I used to do was smoke a little weed?" "How did I gain a hundred pounds before I even knew what was happening?"

Conversely, as we shift our consistency and move the momentum in the other direction, we will be surprised in other ways. "Wow, I've become the top performer in my group or my firm!" Or, "I've been consistent with good eating habits; I didn't think I could lose a hundred pounds, but I did!" Sometimes we improve in areas we weren't expecting, but they manifest because we've made a commitment to improve ourselves. "I haven't thought about it in a long time, but I don't react the way I used to when something bothers me." All these manifestations are real and are a result of consistency and the momentum that ensues.

Can we go from a steady diet of detrimental behaviors to a steady diet of beneficial behaviors overnight? It's very likely that we cannot. "First things first" is very applicable here. There are probably glaring behaviors that need to be addressed first, and then we can move into others as we heal. It's important that we don't overwhelm ourselves by trying to change everything overnight. It's crucial to remember patience in changing our behaviors and ultimately ourselves.

If our dysfunction is characterized by being paralyzed by fear and not moving ourselves forward, maybe we consistently offer ourselves the gift of doing one thing per day that we didn't allow ourselves to do before. Maybe we reach out and speak with a stranger. Maybe we leave the house and spend some time around others. Maybe we show up in person and ask for that job. Maybe we spend less time hiding behind the computer or phone. Remember, to the degree we intentionally decide to do things differently, that is the degree we can expect change to show up in our life. There is nothing outside us that will do it for us. Wishing and hoping bear no fruit. It is only our dedication to doing things differently that will pave the way for real change.

If we have addiction issues, maybe we go to a meeting every day, even if we don't speak with another soul while we're there. Maybe we decide to not eat after 6 pm consistently if we have a food addiction; or call our sponsor/mentor once per day if we find ourselves struggling internally. There's a myriad of things we can do and they all matter. They will all effect a change in us and how we feel if we commit on a consistent basis.

When we start to see changes in ourselves and begin to accumulate some confidence, we can add some other things to do on a consistent basis. After a while we will develop new routines and a new way of living. A new way of living means a new trajectory, and a new trajectory means a new life. This time around, though, as we develop our life by consciously choosing what we're doing, mindfully and intentionally, we have the life that we've chosen and worked for, not the life that our fears, addictions, or neglect have chosen for us. We have a life to be proud of and, more importantly, a life to be grateful for.

Discipline

Discipline is an interesting counterpart to consistency; they coexist as sentries on our journey. They can help keep us from falling back into old behaviors, if we call them up and lean on them as principles to which we adhere to the best of our ability. Discipline is the instrument of our resolve and stands side by side with consistency.

What happens when we don't feel like making that phone call to ask for support? What happens when we're "not in the mood" to work out or pray or meditate? What if it's raining and we don't feel like going to that meeting? Discipline says, "Tough shit, do it anyway."

I've been sober for a long time, and early on my sponsor (or mentor) used to say to me, "The most important time to go to a meeting is when you don't feel like it." I carry that thought process with me today in every aspect of life. What if we don't feel like "adulting" or don't feel like paying our bills anymore? The answer is, "Tough shit." It's not about how we feel in this new life as much as it is about what we're responsible for. In case nobody explained it to us before today: Life doesn't care about how we feel, it's coming down the pike regardless of our feelings.

There is immense reward for us as we learn to say, "Tough shit," to ourselves and do whatever it is that we don't want to do, regardless of how we feel at any given time. If our life is centered around the avoidance of pain or difficulty, we're completely missing the point of our existence. We strengthen, we improve as human beings, and we grow stronger to the extent we face and go through pain and tough times. If there ever was an erroneous belief in our current society as regards developing and improving ourselves, it's that being weak-minded and weak-spirited is okay. I can promise you it's not. Building ourselves on purpose and developing a strength where we don't allow ourselves to get away with mediocrity in mind, body, heart, or spirit, is absolutely crucial.

Does everyone need to reach summit after summit and embrace huge risks and challenges? No, they do not. However, is there an incredible abundance of people out there that don't expect much of themselves? I believe there is. I also believe those same people can change themselves and their lives immensely if they embrace and implement some simple ideas. Simple, not easy.

Let's look at human beings and their development for a moment. We're born as helpless babies, not able to care for ourselves in any way. As we grow and develop, we gain muscle, coordination, strength, and the ability to feed ourselves. We learn, understand, and begin to be able to absorb and fathom what's going on around us, developing resources from which to draw as we mature into our existence. Growth is natural and crucial and is a gift for the first several years of our life. We're not asked to do too much independent thinking as we learn to clothe ourselves, tie our shoes, and attend school. Then, as we move further, it gets a little more difficult. We must make decisions, choose, and learn to either say yes or no to this or that, whatever is put in front of us. This is where our parents, conditioning, and socializing start to make an impact on our life. All of these things matter, but there comes a time when we are faced with the toughest element, regardless of our rearing: responsibility. Responsibility can be embraced and utilized to allow us immeasurable freedom. It can also be ignored and avoided, which will inevitably lead to our demise, either in body, mind, heart, spirit, or all the above.

The short answer to life when we become able to choose and to make decisions for ourselves is, it's all on us. We are responsible for everything. If we want a better, happier life, we're responsible. If we want to quit smoking, we're responsible. If we want to not get so angry all the time, we're responsible. If we want a better job or career, we're responsible. If we need to lose weight, we're responsible.

The shirking of responsibility and making other people or situations responsible for us, or at least responsible for how we feel, is what keeps us stuck. We're not victims, we're not helpless, we're not to be pitied.

Again, I must ask: Why do we see so much mental illness, obesity, and addiction? Why do we see so many people taking pills in a vain attempt to make themselves happier? Why do we see so much acceptance of laziness and apathy? If we've improved as a society, why is there so much crime and callousness and lack of caring for others and their lives? We're not improving as a society if we're not progressing as strong, capable, disciplined, healthy, happy human beings.

It is important to ask ourselves these questions as we decide how much discipline we're going to implement in our own life. It's essential to understand that we will be in the great minority when choosing this path, and it's valuable to recognize that we will be the one to whom true peace, happiness, and fulfillment are earned when we embrace a principled way of living.

The great news is, once we start to apply discipline to ourselves and our everyday affairs, it's almost impossible to go back. If we do go back, there's a lot of pain involved because we've tasted the "other side," and our constitution has a difficult time falling back to obsolete behaviors. This is one of the most wonderful things about growth in all areas of life. There is momentum, there is a force out there that wants us to move forward, to reach new heights, to straighten our trajectory toward our True North or ultimate good. We can continue to improve upon every aspect of ourselves until it's time to trade in the meat costume. I'm not sure what happens after we trade in the meat costume, but I do know, while I'm here wearing it, I want life to be rewarding and fulfilling, including everyone whose life I touch. Before we trade it in, it's important to know deep within ourselves that we contributed, we mattered, and we didn't waste our opportunity. There is no limit to where living by a set of principles can take us.

Faith, patience, determination, consistency, and discipline can be a lonely path. Very few in this world will be willing to look closely at themselves, not to mention, embrace the principles required to effect real change in their life. Again, that's okay. Changing trajectories is daunting and requires intestinal fortitude. In addition, others may not need or have any desire to change, no matter what we think.

Important to keep in mind is to know that we can't do this for anyone else or convince anyone that is not ready. Everyone's journey is their own, and it can be tough to see the ones we love fall into damaging lifestyles and fail to modify themselves, to their own detriment. Most aren't ready for an orderly, principle-driven lifestyle, or, if they've been engaging in destructive behaviors over time, a revision to what they know. The best thing we can do is be an example, and many times that example will be rejected by someone who feels they don't want to change or don't need to change. That's okay too. Often the most effective gift we can offer ourselves is a mindful approach to others by understanding that we cannot effect change in them, but we can be there for them if and/or when they desire change.

CHAPTER EIGHT

OUR SIDE OF THE STREET

W e've been traversing this journey, exploring what we're ultimately searching for in this life and considering what we do and how we do it. There can be no other way to alter our reality, meaning our experience of this life, than examining and, if need be, revising how we approach our every day. We already know that attempting to alter the trajectory of our life through other means such as attention, substances, food, sex, gambling, etc., is futile. We know that allowing ourselves to be stopped by fear only keeps us stuck. We know that it is our responsibility to overcome the encumbrances within ourselves. We not only have an obligation to be better and do better for ourselves, but also for everyone around us.

We can call upon and utilize honesty (especially with ourselves), courage, perseverance, and clarity to begin. These will help put us in the position of understanding that change may be necessary. The first crucial step in our mission. Once we've decided to take that plunge and are steadying ourselves with the understanding that this will be a challenging and, as a result, highly rewarding undertaking, we can call upon other principles, including faith, patience, determination, consistency, and discipline. These will ensure we stabilize ourselves and provide the ballast we will require to get through the tough times and stay on course. The great freedom we begin to internalize will be its own reward at times, and other times, we will just need to hang on with both hands until the storms pass, as they always do.

So how do we know if we're on the right track? How do we know if we're progressing and changing our trajectory?

Early on, this journey can be tough. It may mean less of what we used to call "fun." It may mean some of the people who shared our interest in addictions must be set aside for a while, or forever. It will likely mean many of the things we used to do don't fit in our life anymore. It may even mean family members don't fit into our new way of conducting ourselves. It's all up to our individual circumstances, and these things tend to sort themselves out over time, as we change.

I had a lot of questions when I embarked upon the journey of changing my trajectory and found it very useful to have support and to seek out mentors. People I wanted to be like in terms of their composure, approach to life, and level of serenity. I also wanted them to be on a purposeful and intentional path, so they could relate to and potentially help me through my difficult times.

Accepting that progress can be slow is very useful when it comes to the beginning of our journey. If we are continually moving forward and not falling back into what we know doesn't work, we are progressing, whether we feel it or not. It's easy to judge ourselves early on and be hard on ourselves because we may feel we're doing all this work but not getting anywhere. Welcome to the party. That is normal and will happen for a while.

Here's what I found difficult when beginning this journey at the age of 19. I was reading books and listening to recordings from people who were successful in all areas of life. I was soaking up all this information and thought, "Well, this shouldn't take too long." I absorbed everything I could, did positive affirmations, and thought I'd soon be levitating, perfect, totally at peace, not to mention, wealthy. Well, it didn't quite happen that way.

It's very easy to get caught up in where we want to go as opposed to where we're at. I believe that's healthy to a large extent because we need to have a purpose for the effort we're putting in. Again, it's important to accept that we must bloom where we're planted, wherever that starting point is. I would caution, though, that it's more important to be in the here and now, attending to our responsibilities, which in the beginning are new and unfamiliar, which can make them difficult and time-consuming. I was not familiar with any of the concepts or principles outlined in this book, so I had to learn (and am still learning) them and consistently practice them every day. What I don't remember hearing in the beginning, although it's entirely possible I wasn't listening, are some of the following truths that can serve to take the pressure off trying to be perfect. Here's what won't happen, ever:

- You won't be levitating, at least not anytime soon.

- You won't ever be perfect in thought, word, or deed.

- You will still get impatient.

- You will still get angry.

- You won't always be in a great mood.

- You will have tough times.

- People will still get upset with you, and you will get upset with them.

We can check these off the list of things to beat ourselves up for. We can't, though, use them as excuses to accept mediocrity from ourselves. We must endeavor to improve in every way that is presented to us and in every way that we uncover through exploration. The journey is one of progress, not perfection. It is a journey of willingness and improvement, and there is no culmination. There is no destination where someday we can stop working or stop being willing. It may sound strange to hear, but the beauty of changing our trajectory is in the moments where we act differently; the relationships we grow and cherish along the way; the times where we don't have to beat someone over the head with our opinion; the mornings we wake up without a pit in our stomach; the mornings we wake up with a smile, knowing all is well. A lot goes into having these moments, and they happen more and more frequently the more we practice an intentional way of living.

Some of the signs we're moving in a better direction may include, but are not limited to:

- We're starting to feel a little better about our life and

perhaps less confused about adopting a new way of living.

- The hole that we felt in the middle of us is starting to fill up.

- We are becoming less dependent on what others think of us for our value or self-worth.

- We're starting to understand that we need to be a student, perhaps for a long time, before we can be a teacher.

- We're learning to concern ourselves only with keeping our side of the street clean and not focusing our attention on what others need to do.

- The principles we discuss in this book are starting to make more sense, and we feel like they're commencing, however slowly, to be integrated into us and how we conduct our life.

- We are not as afraid to take a risk, and we have started to do things that we were previously scared to do, even though we still feel fear.

- We are becoming more able to take a deep breath and settle ourselves down.

- Instead of just wanting all the time, we are becoming grateful for the things we have.

- We are starting to think less about ourselves and what we think we need.

If some of these things are coming true for us, which they inevitably will be if we adopt a life based on principle as opposed to what we deem are our momentary needs for "fulfillment," we are absolutely on the right track. We are unquestionably doing it!

I've found in the years I've spent working to improve and move toward a peaceful and productive life, that a sure sign I'm making progress is being suddenly taken aback by the things that just don't hit my radar in terms of mattering any-more. Suddenly something that used to matter will come to mind, and I will just think to myself and chuckle a little because it just isn't relevant or important. Or, one of the sayings or proverbs that made no sense or little sense to me, suddenly deepens in its meaning or has been integrated into my life, without perceivable conscious effort on my part.

For example, the simple phrase, "One day at a time." As I was moving into a different way of living and a different way of perceiving the world, an everyday struggle was not falling prey to my addictions. Just staying sober had all my attention, especially as I tried to wrap my head around staying sober for the rest of my life! At 19, that seemed like an impossible task. I decided to go to college after I got sober, and that was one of the most difficult environments to be in as drinking and drugs flowed freely. This was certainly true in the late 1980s and I'd guess the same today.

People who I relied on for help and advice would say to me, "You only need to stay sober today." Okay, makes sense. I think I can do that. They also said, "When that becomes difficult, you might have to pare that down to a few hours or even a few minutes at a time." Okay, I guess I can try that too. Not easy. Then they said, a little more directly, "If you have one foot in yesterday and one foot in tomorrow, you're peeing all over today. If you're thinking about yesterday, you can be stuck in guilt or regret; if you're thinking about tomorrow, you can be stuck in fear or trepidation." Got it, makes sense. These are all the things I needed to be introduced to early on, just to keep my sobriety intact. Whatever it took at that point to reduce the anxiety and pressure of being sober in a not-so-sober world was helpful.

I have a fast-paced mind, which I guess is a blessing as well as a curse. There are times when things blow through my mind very quickly and then blow out, which in the case of addiction is great when difficult thoughts blow out, but not so fun when they keep blowing in! I needed a reprieve from my mind; something a little more profound than taking things one day or moment at a time.

When I was caught up in my mind, it seemed that everything negative mattered. The losses, the failures, people's opinions were all swirling around in there, with no real way to turn down the noise. Was there a way out? Was there a way to turn off that noise?

It's difficult to understand, especially in the beginning of this journey, that uncertainty is a big part of the process. We get to a point where we have unshakeable faith and resolve, but early on, it is easy to be very affected by what other people might think or say about us.

We need experience to overcome this and learning to quiet our mind plays a big part.

Fortunately, I was able to stay sober through those times and utilizing the tool of taking things a day or a moment at a time seemed to help.

Fast-forward almost forty years later and "One day at a time" has an entirely new meaning to me and to my life. This new meaning is not something I consciously pursued or attempted to drill down and understand. I believe the new understanding came from a willingness to learn and be open to more profound meaning in all areas of my life. The things I couldn't see with my eyes started to be more important to me. As I pursued life with fervor and began to take risks and fail, put myself out there and fail again, I was compelled to, or perhaps more accurately, pushed toward the opposite of a noisy life and a noisy mind. This to me is where Life or God or Higher Power or Great Spirit or whatever we choose to call something greater than ourselves reaches out a hand to assist.

It's important to note here, that we can effect change in our life in the midst of pursuing our other goals and aspirations. There is a synergy that develops when we're working on our body, mind, heart, and soul, simultaneously. As we've explored, we can be out of balance when we're solely looking to improve our financial condition, filling our head with data or facts, or putting muscle on our body. There's a lot more to our trajectory, as we now know. There must be investigation into a well-rounded and comprehensive approach to our life. This is how we grow amid an already demanding life.

This is also where the exploration and conscious, relentless search, come in handy. I started to explore my growing need to have peace and serenity in my mind and heart, amid and because of my exploration. Not to mention jumping into a life with which I was unfamiliar, based on my age as well as my upbringing.

I went from a very blue-collar upbringing and surroundings in the Midwest, to a very white-collar sales position in Boston. From pounding nails for a living to speaking with business owners for a living about a subject that I did not yet understand. Uncomfortable? Yes. Risky? Yes. Scary? Yes.

I had to have something to rely upon that took the bite out of the stress associated with those risks and those changes. I needed a reprieve from the go, go, go lifestyle, where I could retreat, reset, and gather up even a modicum of serenity. "One day at a time" did not cut it anymore, I needed to find something different. It was not a matter of staying sober at that time, it was much more a matter of finding relief.

I bought books on quieting the mind and meditation. I attempted to do what they recommended and started to practice sitting in one place for a few minutes and observing my breath. For a person with a type A personality, easier said than done. I had, at least what I deemed then, low levels of success, not due to the method but due to my inability to quiet myself. They spoke about being in the "present moment" and I just couldn't wrap my head around that. I would try for a period of time and then stop trying. I would look for new methods and try those for a while until finally, I was led to a teacher and mentor that taught me a meditation practice that resonated. Perhaps I became ready for it by the practice I'd done all those years prior. This was over twenty years ago now, so my practice and my understanding of "One day at a time" has gone from trying to stay sober one day or hour or minute at a time, to observing my mind, whilst focusing on a mantra, in the present moment.

The value of the present moment is immense. The value of not being caught up in the debris and the rubble hanging around our mind is paramount to moving forward. It is through this place that we can enter universes unknown, within ourselves. Within the quiet.

The reason I relate this story is because the value of exploring, learning, and being willing to try new things cannot be overemphasized, at least that's how it's worked for me. Did I do the work that was in front of me? Yes, but not all the time. Did I choose the direction that work was going to take me? No, I'm not that smart. Do I ever have any idea of what is next for me as I either do the work or fail to do the work? No, I don't. I can say, though, that when I fail to utilize what I've learned or get off track, I know I'm pushed back on, usually via some kind of pain.

Stagnation in life does not exist. We are either going forward or we are going backward. We are either learning and growing and squeezing ourselves toward a better trajectory, or we are doing the same unhealthy things repeatedly and reaping those results. I don't make the rules. I have just tried to find out what the rules are and align with them as best I can at any given time in my evolution.

It's at this juncture I'd like to discuss possibly the most profound and life-changing feeling we will ever experience. I say "feeling" because it can be something that starts small and grows in us over time, as we consciously pay attention and grow.

It is also a principle because it must start with recognition and practice. It is not easy at first, especially if we've never taken moments to stop and change the ceaseless torrent of activity that our brain provides.

It must be conscious; it must be purposeful. At least in the beginning.

We will not find it in our phone or laptop. We will not find it in our friends or neighbors, but we may call it up because of them. It will not be inherent in the things we've acquired but can certainly be included in what we've earned as well as what we've been gifted.

Its greatest strength can be found in silence and paying attention, this moment. It's the chill down our spine when we're brought to tears by beauty or talent or love.

When we're troubled, there is no better way to lift our mind and heart from the quagmire, consciously migrating our focus.

We will know we're progressing when we begin to call upon its gentle yet torrential power.

Then, as we continue diligently down the path, it begins to traverse the journey with us, part of our very fiber.

We don't take credit for it, or anything. We open our eyes and see the speck that we are. Not in a deprecating or demeaning way. In reality. Do we deserve all this? Maybe. Maybe not.

Gratitude.

CHAPTER NINE

WAIT. DOWNLOAD WHAT?

W e've touched on the idea, or better, the reality, that we operate in this world as a body, mind, heart, and soul. Let's do a deeper dive into each of these aspects of ourselves and how we can improve our relationship with them. This will put us in the best position to truly enjoy as well as thrive in this lifetime.

It is helpful to understand right out of the gate that working to affect every aspect of ourselves and the subsequent manifestation in our world is crucial to our success. When I speak of success, I never mean one area of life. I mean a well-rounded life where we are intentionally influencing and promoting healthy behaviors for ourselves physically (body), mentally (mind), emotionally (heart), and spiritually (soul).

It can be quite a profound wakeup call when we discover, admit, and internalize the indisputable fact that we are constantly influencing either health in these areas or disorder and distress. What we've decided to do every day with our adherence to, or ignorance of, a principle-driven approach, affects every aspect of ourselves. My food intake, exercise regimen, breathing method, quiet time, or lack thereof, quality of relationships, etc., all get downloaded into the complex mechanism called "me," and the output is what is manifesting as my trajectory in this lifetime. So how do we begin to acknowledge the input, so we can change and improve the output? To be more definitive, how do we get our life moving in a direction that gets us what we truly want, our "wishlist," out of our time on this rock?

As we've discussed, the difficulty is not a lack of information or direction, especially in the information-heavy world in which we reside. It's typically fear, unwillingness, or laziness that keeps us stuck. When we decide we want something different, through hitting our bottom or being sick and tired of being sick and tired, we may find ourselves in a position where we open ourselves to learning and, subsequently, changing.

Crucially important to understand is that these aspects of ourselves work in synergy with each other. There is a harmony to being healthy and there is disharmony in being unhealthy, to which each of these facets that make up "us" contributes.

Let's take a look into each of these aspects of ourselves and some ways in which we might affect meaningful changes for ourselves, hence changes for those lives we touch.

Body

This amazing mechanism, which we too often take for granted, carries us from place to place and allows us to see, touch, smell, and taste our beautiful world. If we take the time to plug into, acknowledge, and appreciate the sensations we are so fortunate to be able to experience, we cannot help but be in awe. Do we ever stop to think about how our eyes see? The complexity and wonder of our ears being able to hear birds singing or our loved ones speaking? What about touching tree bark with our fingers or green grass under our feet?

Now imagine those sensations being taken away. What if I lose my sight or my ability to walk or hear? What if my organs begin to fail, or I develop a disease where I am forced to change my lifestyle or undergo debilitating treatments for a prolonged period? These manifestations in our body can certainly awaken us to how we're treating this incredibly valuable gift we refer to as our body.

It's not that we know exactly how everything we do, much less say and feel, affects our body, but we do know that there are commonsense and reasonable ways to treat ourselves that will definitively improve our chances of being healthy for much of our life.

I am an example of what not to do for much of my life, but can also, through experience with the other side of that coin, perhaps offer some ways to turn things around and get on a healthier path. As we've touched on, there is always a cost to what we do for and to ourselves. We are earning where we are in this life and what our trajectory looks like. I earned many of the physical issues I've experienced and have paid the price for not paying attention to how I've treated myself.

When we're young, it's easy to ignore issues and "work through the pain," as many in my generation were taught. I bought into that, and as an athlete for much of my life, I carried the badge of "suck it up" as far as I could before my body started to experience more and more breakdowns. When I was told to stretch, I ignored the advice. When I was told to not throw the baseball too hard before I warmed up, I ignored that advice. I was told that icing my knees and taking ibuprofen were not going to fix them and that I might want to take it a little easier on those joints "because they need to last you a lifetime" while I was playing in four basketball leagues at the age of 35.

"Don't you buy that 28-ounce framing hammer, you idiot! That thing will destroy your elbow and shoulder. It's too heavy," said Johnny, an older carpenter. He looked like his body was pretty beat-up from being a framer his whole life.

"Okay, I gotcha," I replied, as I shrugged off the advice.

I was six feet, six inches tall and about 220 pounds. Feeling indestructible.

I bought the 28-ounce hammer. Found out not too long thereafter, Johnny was right. My elbow and shoulder suffered as I swung that thing hundreds, if not thousands of times per day.

As I grew older, I was told that too much stress or working all the time and not taking a break could be unhealthy. I knew better, or so I thought. How did my escapades of over-indulgence and lack of attentiveness to solid advice work out for me? Not too well.

I've had elbow surgery, three knee surgeries and finally, a knee replacement, shoulder reconstruction, and ulcerative colitis. All from not listening to people who were trying to give me advice based upon their experiences. There have been more things, but these I can directly tie to my inattention and failure to utilize my intelligence, otherwise known to me as "dumbass syndrome" (see my first book, *When I Stop Fighting*).

The good news is, and the news I care about today is that everything that happened—all the not listening, all the not paying attention, all the ignoring of the signs—has driven me to a place where I get incredible joy out of exploring how to be healthy in my body. I earned all my breakdowns and now I am earning the new trajectory I've been on for many years. I can never change the things that have happened, nor do I want to, but I can change how I treat myself moving forward. Bloom where I'm planted, right? It's a lifelong journey and one we can continue to get better at as we gather experience and seek knowledge.

I had no idea how my mind, heart, and soul contribute to the health of my body, and I continue to learn as I go. When I adopt practices in my life that reduce angst, reduce fighting with myself, and promote a clean, resolute mind and a clear conscience, I am improving the health of my body. When I take the time to rest my body and my mind and achieve quiet in my heart and soul, I improve the health of my body.

As I've explored and learned how to treat my body more intentionally and intelligently, I've adopted practices that, to date, have contributed to, at the age of 58, not being on any medications; normal blood pressure; asymptomatic ulcerative colitis; no diabetes or pre-diabetes; and no excess fat.

I mention the tough times as well as the times when the results were better because I want you to know that it's all a part of the process of growth. Had I not had the tough times, I wouldn't have been so open to changing how I've done things. As we've explored, we all come to our crossroads and we all have those moments of clarity, where we know we need to change. I certainly did. I am no different from anyone else. What I finally did was listen and then start to do things in a different way. Doing things in a different way, intentionally, will change our trajectory.

Mind

What is this thing between our ears and what is it used for? Some might call it the brain and believe it's just gray matter, a physical organ that helps us move around, feel pain and pleasure, and solve problems. I agree with that, but I also contend it's much more than that. As discussed in my first book, *When I Stop Fighting*, I am not a doctor, scientist, or anything of the sort. I am, though, someone with a good amount of mileage and experience in paying attention and living intentionally, who'd like nothing more than to share my experience and perhaps help others to an understanding of this life in a deeper, more meaningful, and helpful way. For this reason, I'd like to speak not about the brain, but the mind.

With the advent of social media, and the internet for that matter, people go to their keyboards or their smartphones for what they deem to be knowledge. It also seems reasonable to assume through observation of this world that people equate the things they look up or see on the internet, social media, or the "news" as contributing to their intelligence. I would contend that this is not true, and this is probably the difference, to me, between the brain and the mind.

The brain can read information, memorize, and regurgitate till the chickens come home to roost, and there is certainly a place for that in this world. Some places, mostly what we refer to as "educational" institutions, value this, and when we've read and regurgitated enough of that stuff, we get a piece of paper that says we read and regurgitated a lot of stuff, now we're "smart." I have one of these pieces of paper, but I'm fortunate to have never equated this piece of paper with being intelligent. I am not here to denigrate what is currently known as education, as I do believe it has a place in society. All I would want as regards the current definition of being "educated" or "intelligent" is some actual evidence. Receipts matter. If it's just memorizing and regurgitating, then how do we explain some of the great geniuses of history? We don't know of them because they did well on some tests or quizzes and earned their pieces of paper. I believe there's a little more to the story.

So, if putting a bunch of stuff in our mind isn't "intelligence," then what is intelligence?

I must begin this conversation by answering a question, with a question: What is it about us that assists in solving difficult problems; ruminates on topics; works in the background to help us untangle quandaries; either toughens us or softens us, depending on how we choose to live; is the gatekeeper for what we allow and disallow in our life; empowers us to respond to simple or complex questions, based on our own experiences; is a repository for not only our memories, but how we work throughout our life based in large measure, on those memories; speaks to us when we're on the wrong path; and broadens and deepens our understanding of ourselves when we choose to head toward True North? I contend that our mind is largely responsible for all the above and much more.

We aren't going to chop all this up into little pieces and go back and forth on which pieces are attributable to our brain or mind or heart or soul. That would be for more "educated" persons to discuss, and in my estimation, it's a waste of time. My intent is to help people based on my experience, not get caught up in definitions and minutia. It may make sense here to start with a story.

If you've read my first book, *When I Stop Fighting*, you know much of my story. I'd like to talk here about how I believe my mind evolved, based on my willingness and desire to change my life and grow as a conscious, intentional human being, utilizing the gifts I've been graciously given, to grow in this lifetime to the best of my ability.

I was, in my younger years, an insecure kid. Whether it was nature or nurture, I don't know and really don't care because wherever we're starting this journey is just where we start. Neither blame nor regret changes a thing and, frankly, is a losing battle 100% of the time.

I couldn't look people in the eye; I didn't feel confident in anything about myself; I used my attempts to do well in sports to feel good about myself. Eventually I turned to drugs and alcohol, and everything that was insecure about me intensified. That path lasted several years and moved me quickly in a direction that would have culminated in death or prison, had I not had a moment of honesty with myself and accepted help. This is where the work had to begin.

At first, I had to lean on others as I attempted to navigate my way through the maze of uncomfortable feelings and thoughts that held sway over my mind, hence, over my life. I didn't have confidence in the simplicity of a conversation because I was sure I was wrong about everything, and people would think I was none too smart. I had no way to numb those thoughts or feelings anymore, so I needed to learn, among the legion of other things, to toughen my mind and not allow everything to get to me.

As I embarked on a new way of life, I was met with many defeats and many circumstances beyond my control. I needed to learn that I was only responsible for how I interacted with the world and everyone in it; I was not responsible for how the world and everyone in it decided to interact with me. Read that one again. That is the crux of and one of the first, as well as lifelong, steps toward having a bear trap for a mind. Could I get through my thick skull that I have no control over anyone or anything else? Could I accept that the only person, place, or thing I have control over is me? Finally, could I accept that it takes a lot of work and a lot of time and patience to get to a point where I truly understand this and then even longer to be able to live it?

These and many more questions are the ones I didn't know to ask, very many moons ago. My mind has helped me sort through the queries, sort through the actions to take to grow and change and come out the other side having experienced immense restructuring.

I had no idea that there were things I would hear a time or two, and they'd stick somewhere inside me for the rest of my life, ready to assist me out of a jam or problem, dispensing wisdom at the right time. I had no idea that concepts and precepts that I didn't understand five or ten or twenty years ago would completely resonate that many years later. I didn't know I'd have ideas that would help me write books about my experiences and possibly help others as well.

I didn't know that I had the strength to boot people out of my life that were unhealthy for me. How does that happen when once upon a time my only desire was to be accepted and liked, at all costs? How is it that very few things get hung up in my mind at this time in my life when many years ago, my mind was a cauldron, filled with agonizing thoughts and rent-free tenants?

I impart my experiences because someone else imparted their experience and helped me get through the mush that used to be my mind and shaped it into something else. Just when we think we're the only ones experiencing difficulty or that no one knows how arduous life is for us, we find out that we're not alone. Everyone goes through varying degrees of difficulty and there are some who get through it and can help others sort through the quagmire. It is helpful to know that we're not alone and that there are actual things that can be done to assist our efforts to strengthen our mind and how our mind relates to the world around us.

To take the discussion of our mind further, I do believe that we can plug into a larger mind, a Universal Mind, that wants to help us navigate the maze known as our life and be successful doing it.

How many times have we been working on a problem or a project and had an idea come "out of nowhere" that we'd never had before that solves our problem? Where the heck does that come from? Do we ever take a moment to ponder that? Where do inventors and the great minds in history get their ideas? It's almost like the ideas are floating out there somewhere, and they just need to be snatched out of the ethers and acted upon. I'm not saying that we're looking to be like Einstein or Tesla or DaVinci. I'm just saying that our mind is much more capable and available to us than we might realize.

We can make tough decisions, we can change ourselves, we can decide for or against things that are good for us and not good for us. Our mind is there to guide us along and help us discern. All we must do is not allow our brain to get in the way.

Heart

Our proverbial heart, also known as our emotional state, is where we meet with everyone else in this world. We've already looked at the fact that in a general sense, we have the same emotions as everyone else on the planet. Happiness, fear, surprise, contentment, anger, amusement, embarrassment, awe, etc. We all get the idea because we all feel these things. The difference is, how do we go about our life either feeling, trying not to feel, or acting/not acting on what is going on in our heart at any given time?

What would it be like to experience anger and not lash out or feel the need to hurt someone else because we're hurting? What would it be like to feel contentment much of or all the time? What if embarrassment was not something that hit our radar, or if it does, we respond with a chuckle as opposed to shrinking into the landscape?

It's important to know that, as we mature, if we mature, we can spend a lot more time in awe, gratitude, and contentment than we spend in anger, fear, and annoyance. Now please understand that there is a very real possibility that we will feel the complete array of emotions throughout our entire life. I would never suggest that at some point we only feel the emotions that feel good. That would be unrealistic and there is a reason and a point to every emotion we feel. Fear can drive us to save ourselves or others, or flee when the time is right. It can also move us toward a better version of ourselves. Perhaps shame helps us be a better person going forward. If we're ever disappointed in ourselves, maybe we decide to not repeat the behavior, or we help someone else avoid a similar mistake.

When I speak of maturity, I don't believe there is a time frame associated with it. We all, God willing, get older but that does not mean that we all mature, especially at the same or a similar rate as others. Some will numb themselves their entire life with mind- or mood-altering substances—illicit, prescription drugs, or otherwise—and never mature to where they would if they felt and responded to life without those crutches. Sadly, little do they know how grand a life without the numbing can be. There may be a blunting of difficult emotion that accompanies their lifestyle, but what about the contentment, awe, and satisfaction they're missing out on? The same can be said for other addictions, as the purpose of the addiction is to satisfy the addiction, not to live a life where the heart leads. Addiction consumes life, so it would be impossible for an actively addicted person to separate from the addiction and experience their heart in a way that those who aren't addicted can.

Now the good news for those who choose to shed addiction as a way of life—Once they embrace the possibility that there is a different, better way, the capacity for living a life from the heart is greatly enhanced. Appreciation, awe, and gratitude are profound in those who accept and consciously pursue another path. I've seen a lot of that and have experienced it myself. Once some of the rewards are realized, they're enhanced by further exploration and progress, and grow continually deeper and more profound over time.

Growth in this realm can then take on a life of its own as we continue to expand and move forward in the life of our heart. This is where joy wells up, sometimes for no apparent reason; this is where gratitude can begin to be the driving force in our life, as we learn to appreciate what we have and, simultaneously, as our desires fade into the background; this is where we're profoundly affected when we see others happy and doing well in their lives. The rewards are great, but they can't be measured; they can only be felt by those who experience them. Can we stop and pay attention long enough to feel the appreciation for a starlit night? Do we truly enjoy seeing other people succeed and experience great things in their lives?

Our heart is vitally connected to our body and our mind. There must be a synergy between all these aspects of ourselves, as we cannot experience the profound nature of the heart if we are poisoning our body or poisoning our mind with the everyday, mainstream, mundane, "just like everybody else" input. How does my body react over time if I eat a lot of fast food or have poor sleeping habits due to late-night binging on food, sugar, etc.? How does my mind grow and become a "bear trap" if I consume a lot of news, politics, or gossip? The answer to these questions is, "Not well." The body and mind contribute to the experience, growth, and ultimate wellness of the heart, and vice versa. I must say again that I'm not the one that makes the rules. I'm here to report from my own experience what has helped me overcome some of the obstacles to the necessary synergy for a fully formed life.

As you may have gleaned from some of my stories, any evolution I've experienced has been by graduating several times (because I was held back for poor performance) from the school of "being an idiot." I've been the guy who has done most things wrong, but I'm also the guy who has paid the piper for those transgressions and done my best to change course. If we're not continuously exploring how to get better and digging deep to find out why we consistently "don't feel good" in our body, hence, our mind, our heart will never get to a place where we wake up in the morning with a smile on our face.

It's incumbent on us, every day, to find out what's holding us back. What's keeping us from feeling good? What's keeping us from being grateful on a consistent basis? Chances are, it's something we're either avoiding or consciously not paying attention to, that could be a catalyst for change. That voice inside us knows what we need to do. That voice inside us can get us started in a direction, should we choose to listen. Truly listening and internalizing means being compelled to act. What's stopping most of us? The failure to act.

We see a lot these days of people purporting they know how to help others with their lives. We see the "experts" all over social media who will let us know how to be financially free, insanely happy, reach our deepest latent potential, and more! The only problem is, many of them haven't figured it out for themselves yet. How a person teaches something they haven't experienced has always been interesting for me to observe. I applaud the enthusiasm and the effort, but experience matters. Going through the ringer and coming out the other side changed, because of tough experiences, takes time, effort, and patience, among many other things. I can't teach what I haven't experienced, which is why I am adamant that I can provide context and experience, as well as teach, because I've been there.

My heart has been damaged, beat up, kicked around, and has become stronger because of intimate experience with doing things wrong, but also a desire and willingness to explore how to do things differently. That's the magic potion, the secret formula for comprehension at the level of the heart. The heart will not morph or mature because of what we read in books; it will not dispense its bounty because of reading some tweets or blogging about emotions. The heart will respond to experience, to change, to willingness to do things differently. The heart will respond to the voyage. How else do we begin to live our life from the perspective of appreciation? How else do we find our way to gratitude? In my experience, we find our way there by going down the wrong roads, making the wrong choices, and doing the wrong things. As we experience consequences, we are faced with choices. If we decide not to change, then … nothing changes, and we face more consequences.

Or, we choose an alternate route. Then we can begin to change. When we choose previously unexplored paths, we begin to experience the joy that can come from these new commitments and our life changes even more. As we resolve to amend ourselves, perhaps we consciously decide to stay away from drugs or alcohol; get off the "happy pills"; lose weight; seek help for other addictions; face our fears or whatever we know is stopping us—and our hearts respond. Our hearts will heal and expand our capacity for honoring and cherishing our life, intentionally. At this juncture, we've transformed our trajectory to a new bearing for the rest of our life, as we've chosen to live in a conscious way.

Soul

Our soul, or spirit, is the seat of our being. It's the wellspring from which all that is beautiful, poignant, and ultimately true, flows. I experience, as I write these words, a stirring inside me, as my soul longs to be welcomed to the surface. The soul is not like the mind or the heart. It's something much deeper, much more profound. We can't think in or with our soul, and we can't feel with our soul, at least in the usual sense. We can't train it like we can train our mind or our body; we can't affect it like we can affect our heart, by doing the "wrong" or the "right" things. It doesn't grow or change or morph or transform. All the work we do to alter our trajectory, or all the work we fail to do to alter our trajectory, will not affect the soul in any way. Our soul is enduring, spaceless, unaltered, unaffected. What does that mean?

It means that we can't learn our soul, we can't move our soul, we can't heal our soul.

We can only *experience* our soul.

When we think of our soul, what comes to mind? Timeless, limitless, ethereal? Can we touch those places? Can we get "there"? I believe we can although it's not "us" getting "there"; it's us allowing, opening, and making room for our soul to join us on the journey we call our life. How does that happen? We move out of the way. We prepare the ground; we quiet the storms; we seek solitude and quiet.

Our soul is not reachable through the noise of our mind. It will not emerge to join us when our heart is turbulent. There is work necessary to prepare the ground. There must be surrender, there must be not-knowing, there must be an understanding that there is something greater than us and an acceptance that we cannot complete this journey on our own, left to our own devices. In most cases, if we allow ourselves an honest look, it will become abundantly apparent that we are not in charge, nor should we desire to be.

Does this mean "God" or something religious? In my understanding of soul and of what I'm imparting, I'd say that it's whatever our understanding is at any given time in our development. Do we need to believe in God to move into this realm of experiencing soul? Not necessarily. Do we need to believe that there is something greater than us out there as a starting point on this path? Yes, we do. It could be Mother Nature; it could be the Universe. It doesn't require us to believe as anyone else believes. In my experience, as we explored previously, my understanding of something greater than me traversed many iterations and continues to expand in breadth and depth. That's just the nature of the journey; it's a trajectory playing out and continuing to move forward. It's nothing to be intimidated by; it's nothing to fear; it's nothing to be concerned about. Once the journey is commenced and committed to, it takes on a life of its own and continues to show us the way, especially in the realm of the soul.

Where once we were rebelliously and joyously in the way, we begin to understand the self-defeating nature of such folly. Where once we thought noise and contention were the path, we begin to embrace that there may be more meaningful answers elsewhere.

We begin the path of exploration, we commence the journey of finding our way to "that place," where quiet is the answer, where we can be "away," if even for a short time, as often as possible. Perhaps it's the feeling of a light breeze across our cheek for a few moments; perhaps it's truly listening to the leaves as they move with the wind and against each other; perhaps it's stopping long enough to experience the aroma of the woods. There are a thousand ways to connect to this moment. There are a thousand ways to embark on a path of mindfulness, where we allow ourselves to experience our soul.

There's an overabundance of noise, angst, contention, and opinions in this world that can be grating, unnerving, and depressing. Are we constantly plugged into the noise? Are we a part of the contention, distress, and ceaseless opinions? If so, we might want to check in to how that makes our life feel and how it affects where we've been and where we're headed. There is no quiet, there is no peace in these places, and they do nothing to move our life forward, at least in the ways we've been discussing. If we're caught there, our trajectory will not improve, and we will continue to deteriorate. Sometimes to snap out of it, we need an event to help us decide that we want something different and better for ourselves. Sometimes, perhaps all we need to do is change our mind about our trajectory. Sometimes that change can spark a new or previously forgotten sense of appreciation or gratitude.

The practice of gratitude can also do for us what we previously thought only the realization of our desires could: It allows us to experience contentment. What is gratitude and how does it move us toward contentment?

As we've explored, embracing quiet, embracing this moment, can move us closer and closer to the experience of our soul. Gratitude is powerful and has to do with true appreciation, but it also allows and provides us with another profound benefit: It takes us out of wanting something in the future and it takes us out of regretting something in the past. If we're truly experiencing gratitude, we're in this moment, we are in the "now." If we're stuck in wanting things or feeling guilt or regret, we're attached to either the future or the past. If we're grateful for something, we're in the present moment and that's all there is. There is no past and there is no future in these moments.

Practicing gratitude starts with actual practice. Perhaps I'm grateful that my eyes can see; perhaps I'm grateful for the warmth of the sun; perhaps I'm grateful that I simply have enough food to get me through the day. Whatever we are grateful for can be practiced every day. That grateful feeling will begin to expand into other areas of our life and may include family, friends, experiences, whatever. The key is to be thankful, which in turn, places us in the moment.

Eventually, gratitude becomes an integral part of our every day. Many times now, I see a sunset or think about how wonderful life is, at any given moment, and I whisper a simple, "Thank you." Very often that will spark a feeling to run down my spine that I can only call "gratitude."

What else can we glean from a practice of gratitude? We begin to learn that to experience a more profound, contented life, we must be less interested in ourselves and what we think we need. If our life revolves around our next stimulation, substance, or desire, we're not truly living. To be driven by only our wants is to be driven by everything outside of us, at the expense of what we could be cultivating inside of us. Gratitude takes us away from that self-imposed trap and allows us to enter moments. Moments of thankfulness, moments of now, moments of experiencing what's real.

It's a profound place to be when our desires are minimal, and we become less concerned with our moment-by-moment "needs." What we think we need is usually not what we need. As we plug into the experience of our soul, we are led to what moves us toward our intentions and our highest good.

Are there other ways to experience our soul? Are there other ways to cultivate quiet and propagate being in the present moment? There are. Perhaps the discovery of a daily meditation practice would be helpful. Perhaps the discovery of an intentional breathing practice or other mindfulness practice would deepen our experience of the soul. It is up to us to explore. Like everything else we've discussed in this book, it's our responsibility and our choice as to whether we discover and embrace practices that will change our trajectory. The experience of our soul will, without doubt, move us nearer and nearer to a True North trajectory.

CHAPTER TEN

ROUTE 66

W hat would happen if we all embraced this journey and decided to apply what's been discussed? How could our life look if we took complete responsibility and embarked upon the path of intentional change? Two years from now? Five years from now? Twenty years?

I already know what's behind me, even though it's been a very long time. Almost forty years of intentionally and consciously working to improve, and I can say with complete abandon that I have no desire to tread where I've already been. I don't want to repeat the past, but more important-ly, I don't want my past to be my future. Well, how could my past be my future? How would anyone know what's in the future? If we don't decide to consciously change, that's how we know what's in our future. What's worse, if we don't change our trajectory and we keep doing what we've been doing, what we've been doing will morph to something more damaging, and our southerly trajectory will only steepen.

Is this what we want? If we know there's a better way, which all of us innately do, then probably not. This is where we need to put our proverbial foot down and decide once and for all that we are going to earn ourselves a better, brighter, and happier future. Why not? We know what's behind us, and we now know that what's behind us is always going to be in front of us, worsening, unless we suck it up for a while and do something about it.

Perhaps the most difficult thing for me, when I was presented with an opportunity to change, was that I had no idea what was on the other side. What the hell would life be like without doing dumb shit with all my crazy friends and without getting drunk or high at every available opportunity? What happens as we change and as we progress? I will attempt to give some mile markers here. Some things that will start to appear as your journey commences. And some things that you can look forward to as you continue through many years, or even decades, of intentional, conscious living.

At first, it's scary to think about what lies ahead; then it's scary to do things differently. It was for me. I had no idea what life might be like by doing things differently. None of us do. All we might be able to reference is the promise from those who have consciously improved themselves. If we're fortunate enough to have even one of those people in our life, we should listen. By "fortunate" I mean get off your ass and go search out a mentor and listen to what they have to say. In my first book, *When I Stop Fighting*, I outlined some of the things you should look for in a mentor. I spoke about Budd, my mentor, who helped set the stage for me by presenting me with ideas and concepts with which I was previously unfamiliar. These helped provide me with a direction in which I could then take the reins and embark upon my own journey of moving my life forward from there. I am hoping my books provide that direction to those desirous of change.

There can be great fear associated with changing ourselves. It helps if we're also motivated by being ready to change, as that might help us push through the fears that will inevitably present themselves. Another way to push past those moments of fear, as previously mentioned, is understanding that "this too shall pass" because it always does, as well as one that's helped me through the years: "Feel the fear and do it anyway."

The mile markers are in no particular order, as I have no clue where anyone is on their journey. Things are going to happen more quickly for some than others, and the path is going to be different for everyone. As we move forward, though, we are going to experience different and incredible things, many we're not expecting. As we traverse the new road, the new "stuff" can be intimidating, but also incredible.

Imagine a trip down Route 66, having never traveled out of your hometown of Bloomington, Illinois. You're going to see huge rivers, plains, the Rocky Mountains, incredible expanses of desert, and then you finally get to Santa Monica, California, the Pacific Ocean. Perhaps you had ideas of what these things might look like but could never capture how you'd be moved and changed, until you experienced them. This is exactly how it works when we consciously and intentionally move ourselves forward in this life, relentlessly. My advice here is to open, welcome, and embrace the changes, as they come. It's from this place that your life will unfold, bloom, and flower.

One of the first things we'll experience, once we've pushed through those fears a few times, is that it gets a lot easier to do it again and again. The freedom that we will begin to experience in these victories can be enormous and will enliven us to continue. Many times, the results will be apparent as perhaps we've taken that risk or started to address our addiction, or perhaps lost some weight. These are all great victories for us, and the hope is that they'll continue to drive us forward. I know in my life, the times I've been able to gain momentum are incredibly rewarding and very useful as they've provided me with the motivation to want more. Momentum is also exactly as promised, which means we can, at some point, take our foot off the gas just a little bit as good habits replace bad ones, and we get more and more comfortable with a new way of living. The fear gets replaced by desire to continue, and at some point, the fears diminish to a point where they lose their teeth. This takes time, effort, and commitment, but it can and does happen.

At another mile marker, we may begin to embrace the fears associated with not just healing but improving in ways we never thought possible. When we're past the difficult, every-day wrestling match known as our addiction(s), trepidations, phobias, whatever it is that had been stopping us, maybe we're ready to move to a new occupation, start a business, ask for that promotion, or be vulnerable and connect with that other person. We might be ready to move into an entirely new experience of life, where we take the risks, learn brand-new skills, or create new disciplines for ourselves. I can promise everyone reading this, that if your new commitment to life is the perpetual cultivation of growth and change, you will inevitably reach all these mile markers, and many more.

We will be more conscious about how we live and the things we choose to do or not do. When presented with the temptation to reverse course and head back down the wrong roads, we'll be able to stop, think, and choose wisely, in the best interest of our body, mind, heart, and soul. At some juncture, we'll find it is no longer possible to choose self-destruction. We'll garner a strength we had never before known. As we integrate and embed that sturdiness, our resolve to continue will be reinforced.

What would happen if the things that used to matter to us lose their allure? I use the word "allure" because many times, when we're on the path of continuous struggle, there's an allure to difficulty and problems, as we previously explored. Being able to point at our "difficulties" somehow takes away our responsibility to change. "But it's hard" or "You have no idea" are the battle cry of those who are best friends with their "issues," instead of themselves.

What if that went away? What if things perceived as problems became opportunities, or better yet, were understood as just "life," and not judged as either good or bad. Wouldn't that be something? It's there (or I should say, it's here) for the unfolding. It's here for those who do the work to uncover themselves and uncover some of the true secrets of living an intentional, conscious way of life.

At some juncture, we'll begin to really understand and internalize the fact that everyone's trajectory is their own. The concept of "keeping my side of the street clean" will rule our days and our actions. We'll be ready to help or assist anyone that is trying, but we don't insert ourselves to "change the world" any longer. There is a wonderful sense of freedom when we do our best every day to brighten the lives of others but also understand that we cannot change anyone that is not ready and willing to change. Just as our trajectory won't be changed by others, nobody's trajectory will be affected by us, unless we're invited in. This includes family. As we embrace that freedom, our life continues to heal and expand. Our work on ourselves and the example we set in becoming a different version of ourselves will prove to be a catalyst for some to want to change.

We'll begin to understand, as we continue to do the work, that the pain and difficulty we've experienced before and after our willingness to change was absolutely necessary. Each step in our process was vital to get us to where we are now. Regret about past mistakes will begin to fade as guilt and shame are replaced with gratitude for everything that brought us to where we are.

"Do you ever regret going down the path you went down in your younger years?" my wife, Kristina, asked me early on in our relationship.

"Not a bit of it," I replied. "I couldn't be where I am now, without everything that happened."

I mean that very sincerely. "Couldn't." Who knows where I'd be if one decision was different, or one bad choice was taken out of the hundreds or thousands of choices made? I don't, and I don't want to find out.

This is where gratitude pops its head in again as we grow and begins to expand throughout our every day. Gratitude for pulling out of the tough times, no matter what they were. Gratitude for being here, now. Gratitude for all the dumb things I did to get me here. Gratitude for what's to come. Gratitude for … (your turn).

How would life be if we were no longer bothered by annoy-ances that would previously rule our days and, hence, our life? What if all of that, or at least most of it, went away as we progress? What if we started to truly not care if our coffee wasn't perfect at our favorite coffee place? Can we shrug off having to have things be convenient or comfortable all the time? If we're truly making progress in our life, we won't need everything, or anything for that matter, to be perfectly aligned with our expectations. In fact, our expectations of what we think we need to be happy will start to go away. What we thought would make us content, makes us miserable, because those expectations can never be fulfilled to our satisfaction. Our getting everything we expect in the way we expect it is just not how life works. When life becomes just a series of stuff that happens, that we can't orchestrate or control, nor desire to orchestrate or control, we're getting somewhere. The freedom we will enjoy when petty things aren't ruining or even impacting one millisecond of our serenity is boundless.

I've been a driven person my entire life. My reasons for being driven have morphed from being incredibly concerned about what others thought of my performance, to now, for the most part, being only concerned with what I think about my performance. I would look at everything as either a "failure" or a "success." I didn't know that there was any other way to perceive the world. When I embarked on a path of self-improvement, it was even more pronounced. I now, or so I thought, had a lot to make up for and a lot to prove. I would be out there in the world trying like hell and mostly failing, sometimes succeeding, or at least based on the definitions I had then. I guess the big question that I wasn't aware of back then was, "Is there a way to look at life from something other than a failure-versus-success perspective?" There is.

I was fortunate to be presented with the very foreign concept, at least to me at that time, and the oft-used cliché, "It's about the journey, not the destination." Well, come to find out, it really is about the journey, but let's take that a step further. What if the defining standard I use for my life is whether I'm doing the best I can? What if that is where the "success" or "failure" is defined? It's easy to get hung up on the destination, but the destination is also where we have no control whatsoever. We can do our best, and there might still be a thousand things that derail us. How can we either pat ourselves on the back or beat ourselves up when the results are not something we control? So, what is it that we do, in fact, control?

We control what we do and how we do it. As it relates to this voyage between birth and death, we decide about us. We decide who we want to be, who our friends are, which tasks we tackle, how we treat our body, mind, heart, and soul, and how we manage our occupation and our relationships. Isn't that enough? Isn't that a sizable enough job to take on without having to also worry about how the end product works out? It's a huge job and one worthy of being deemed a smashing success when we go about it in a way that promotes an effective and flourishing life.

We're not always going to win. In fact, we'll lose more than we win if we stick our nose in enough new experiences. Let's start defining "success" as putting in our best efforts and define "failure" as putting in paltry or no effort. We'll leave the results up to a universe better equipped to handle it.

We will begin to truly welcome challenge and even difficulty as we continue on this route. Do we want everything to be as hard as it was when we were just starting to move into a new way of life? No, of course not. But we will start to look for different and even more hearty challenges as we go. We won't shy away from what might stretch our current capabilities, and we'll want to continue to improve and expand our life.

At some juncture along this route, we'll begin to feel like we're being led. We'll develop a belief system that has room for things we had not heretofore entertained. We'll develop faith in something other than ourselves. The scope of what we believe is possible will broaden and deepen. Our attitude about the world and its inhabitants will transform into a softer and more manageable place. The fighting will lessen and eventually stop. We will calm.

The last mile marker I'd like to explore is the idea of getting to a point where we are not really concerned with ourselves, which is where true freedom resides. I know it sounds weird, but let's dive in a little deeper.

We spend our life telling ourselves various things. Not just things but things about ourselves: I'm too tall; too short; pretty; smart; dumb; handsome; thin; fat; too old; too young; etc. What does this mean? It means that we spend an incredible amount of time worried about ourselves. Self-focused. Self-centered. We all understand this because we all either do it or have done it. It's exhausting.

What would happen if we didn't have to think about or worry about ourselves all the time, or at least not as much as we do now? What if we adopted some of what we've discussed in this book into our life and really started to feel great about what we do, as opposed to what we want or how we think we appear? We deal with what we can control, which we now know is only ourselves, and we commit to doing the absolute best job we can with that project. We won't have time to worry about all that isn't happening or all that we desire because we'll be doing the work! The results will take time, but they will also speak for themselves.

The more we do to move ourselves and our life forward, the more we'll forget about what we think we need or what we think will make us happy. It's truly amazing how it works, but I promise you it does. We can then spend our time on more worthy pursuits.

When we've made the commitment to ourselves and the advancement of our body, mind, heart, and soul, there will be new versions of ourselves waiting around every corner. Maybe we adopt new nutritional guidelines; times we allow ourselves to eat and times we don't; or perhaps a cleansing or fasting schedule as we move forward.

Maybe we read new types of books that feed our curiosity about what's possible in this lifetime, so that we can adopt new practices; or we set up weekly calls with a mentor to learn how they improved themselves. Maybe we go out and practice engaging with people with whom we're unfamiliar, to continue to move through our trepidations.

What if we committed to being conscious about all our words and deeds, ensuring we hurt no one intentionally, or to the best of our ability, unintentionally? Or we very intentionally let people know how we feel about their support and love. Maybe we rid our life of more and more of the toxic people who inevitably have tagged along for the ride, sometimes for our entire life.

Perhaps along the way we deepen our understanding of a power greater than ourselves and adopt beliefs that have an impact on us. If we've explored the value of solitude and quieting the noise that can be an inevitable part of life, maybe we've been led to a practice of meditation that makes sense for our path. Maybe we've incorporated a daily practice of gratitude and have begun to live in moments. Perhaps searching out a practice of conscious breathwork.

There are myriad ways to improve, move ourselves forward, and thrive. What we must do is get curious, explore, commit, practice, flail, change, lather, rinse, repeat.

Life can be: waking up every day with a smile and contentment that we currently do not experience; a feeling of thankfulness for every day; not being overwhelmed by fear or regret; a welcoming of all experiences, regardless of difficulty; embracing and enjoying risk; nothing and no one living rent-free in our head or heart; tranquility about who we are and how we fit in this world; peace within which surpasses our understanding; mental toughness like a bear trap; a no bullshit policy that emanates from our being; focus like a laser.

Do these things sound like a life you'd like to live?

Does this sound like the manifestation of our "wishlist"?

Then, from wherever we are currently, and whatever our trajectory is, let's start, let's change, let's begin, or begin again.

With Gratitude

Thank you so much for reading my book!

If you've enjoyed my first two books:

WHEN I STOP FIGHTING: The Unexpected Joy of Getting My Head Out of My Ass

and/or

WHEN YOU STOP FIGHTING: The Road You're On is Your Own Asphalt

or you feel they may have helped you, or could help someone you know (or someone you don't know),

Please leave me a **great review** on **Amazon** or **Goodreads**, or both, so we can continue to spread the word! Thank you!!

Let's Stay in Touch!

Twitter @DarylEDittmer

https://twitter.com/DarylEDittmer

Facebook When I Stop Fighting

https://www.facebook.com/profile.php?id=100095169161814

Instagram whenistopfighting

https://www.instagram.com/whenistopfighting/

Tik Tok @Theunexpectedjoys

https://www.tiktok.com/@theunexpectedjoys

YouTube @WhenIStopFighting–ThePodcast

https://www.youtube.com/channel/UC9xdob7W6Jf4cv97Z7f4qiQ

Resources

There have been many resources, books, and teachers that have assisted me over the years. Here are a few. Many are from the earlier years in my journey, and some are more recent. My hope is that they will help you, wherever you are in your journey:

https://www.breathonance.com founded by Amit Anand, M.D.

Ageless Body, Timeless Mind by Deepak Chopra, M.D.

The Greatest Salesman in the World by Og Mandino

The Lost Booklets of Emmet Fox

The Power of Myth by Joseph Campbell

The Ten Commandments by Emmet Fox

Awareness is Evolution by Kali J. Banks

The Richest Man in Babylon by George S. Clason

Jonathan Livingston Seagull by Richard Bach

Think and Grow Rich, by Napoleon Hill

As a Man Thinketh by James Allen

The Road Less Traveled by M. Scott Peck, M.D.

Tao Te Ching by Lao Tzu

The Seven Spiritual Laws of Success by Deepak Chopra, M.D.

Awaken the Giant Within by Tony Robbins

The Art of War by Sun Tzu

Way of the Peaceful Warrior by Dan Millman

The Healing Power of Mindfulness by Jon Kabat-Zinn

The Art of Happiness by Dalai Lama

The Miracle of Mindfulness by Ticht Nacht Han

The Power of Positive Thinking by Dr. Norman Vincent Peale

Made in United States
Troutdale, OR
12/02/2024